GEORGE
BEST

A LIFE IN THE NEWS

Best's genius confounds Arsenal at Highbury

By David Lacey : Arsenal 0, Manchester United 2

What should have been one of Manchester United's hardest games of the season turned out to be one of their easiest victories. Arsenal, lacking Ure, and with Neill not fully fit, were ill equipped to deal with Best, a point he emphasised in the second half with a goal of rare audacity and skill. Charlton's absence seemed utterly irrelevant, as indeed did Arsenal's unbeaten home run of 27 League and Cup games. More pertinently perhaps, they have yet to win a First Division game this year.

The match could have given Arsenal a boost of confidence for what will surely be the club's most important fortnight of the season so far—the League Cup final against Leeds United at Wembley on Saturday, followed by their FA Cup fifth round tie against Birmingham City at Highbury a week later, but it only served to confirm any lingering doubts about the present side's lack of ability at the highest level.

Ingenuous style

There were moments when it seemed that Arsenal's ingenuous style, based on everybody's willingness to run, challenge and make something out of the most unlikely situations, would bring rewards that their lack of skill denied them. Early in the game, for instance, Simpson headed the ball to Armstrong and met the return with a soaring volley that might have made all the difference to the outcome had it gone a foot lower. Just before half time Gould and Sammels went equally close but this was the sum of Arsenal's attacking threat ; the rest of the time Graham and Gould were stifled by Sadler and Stiles.

Manchester United's performance was a masterpiece of controlled pace underlying the skill and ingenuity which make them what they are. An hour of aggression based on depth in defence and tenacity in midfield was followed by a gentle run-down in the last 30 minutes, when, with the match safe, wind and limb were preserved for Gornik on Wednesday.

The cold, and possibly the pros-

the efforts of McLintoch, Armstrong and Sammels to create some kind of cohesive movement in the Manchester half. Law performed this type of limited but effective rôle for the Rest of the World against England in the FA Centenary match at Wembley in 1963 ; from all accounts Scotland needed a similar feat on Saturday.

Inevitably Best stole the show. Last week his boutique business won a £15,000 mail order contract and Arsenal were unlucky enough to be first in line for the celebration. He stayed upfield and poor Storey was given Ure's job of shadowing him ; as the game wore on it became more a case of Best marking Storey. After 23 minutes they both went for a long clearance from Stepney, which landed some way out on the right wing. It was not imediately clear what happened next. Best was on Storey's outside, and suddenly the ball came flying back towards the far corner of the Arsenal goal. Furnell, taken by surprise could not get to it. An own-goal, it transpired, although at the time one quite believed that Best had hooked the ball in from an impossible angle.

Ten minutes after the interval however, he scored a goal that brooked no argument. Kidd centred from the left, Law met the ball near the penalty spot, an nodded it down to Best's feet. Wit the Arsenal defence massed i front of him Best dummied to th right, swerved inwards, turne round, took the ball two pac through a gap that he ha opened up to his left and hit it in the top right hand corner of th net.

The rest of the game was play out in stunned silence on the pa of the Arsenal supporters, punc ated at intervals by the squeals those young Manchester support who see Best as a Beatle in fo ball boots.

Arsenal.—Furnell : Storey, McNab, McLintock, Neill, Simpson ; Jenkins, Go Graham, Sammels, Armstrong.

Manchester United.—Stepney ; Dun Burns, Crerand, Sadler, Stiles ; Best, K Fitzpatrick, Law, Aston.

Referee.—D. J. Lyden 'Birmingham'.

OLYMPIC GAMES

Africans stumble

GEORGE BEST

A LIFE IN THE NEWS

from the pages of the
Guardian and the *Observer*

edited by Richard Williams

theguardian

The Observer

Aurum

First published 2006 by
Aurum Press Ltd, 25 Bedford Avenue, London WC1B 3AT
www.aurumpress.co.uk
in association with Guardian Books.
Guardian Books is an imprint of Guardian Newspapers Ltd

Introductory material copyright © 2006 by Richard
Williams

The pieces collected in this book were first published in the
Guardian or the *Observer*.

A catalogue record for this book is available from the
British Library.

ISBN-10: 1 84513 201 7
ISBN-13: 978 1 84513 201 9

10 9 8 7 6 5 4 3 2 1
2010 2009 2008 2007 2006

Designed and typeset in Bell MT and Helvetica Neue by
SX Composing DTP, Rayleigh, Essex

Printed and bound in Great Britain by MPG Books,
Bodmin, Cornwall

This book is printed on paper certified by the Forest
Stewardship Council as coming from a forest that is well
managed according to strict environmental, social and
economic standards.

Introduction

So much was written about George Best in the 30 years separating the end of his career as a footballer from his death in 2005 that the real substance of his life – in other words, what he actually did on the pitch during the few short years between ignition and burnout – is in danger of becoming buried in the mudslide of picaresque anecdote and lachrymose lamentation, or reduced to a repertoire of no more than half a dozen frequently replayed video clips. Even those of us who saw him in his prime sometimes find ourselves needing to wipe the screen of memory in order to remove a dusty residue from mental images of a slender youth flickering across the field, aflame with impudence and ambition.

What we have between these covers, by contrast, is the pristine clarity of the real-time story. Taken from the pages of the *Guardian* and the *Observer*, these pieces comprise a direct record of Best's time in the public eye, committed to print by a group of gifted journalists whose sense of personal involvement in the unfolding tale becomes increasingly clear. With Best, that was the way of it: whatever vicissitudes he encountered – and sometimes provoked off the pitch, to see him at play with a ball was to be reminded of what, in our hearts, we hoped the game could be. The sense of protectiveness he inspired in sports reporters would be mirrored, of course, by the emotions he engaged in his wives and girlfriends; both sides of his appeal are reflected here.

It is the football, however, that takes precedence, and in reading through the accounts of his early days there is a special pleasure for me in retrieving for posterity some of the work of Albert Barham and Eric Todd, two men whose match reports for the *Guardian* in the 1960s convinced a beginner still in his teens that football matches could be described not just with clarity and accuracy (the two cardinal virtues) but with colour, wit and sensitivity. Other distinguished contributors, including Hugh McIlvanney, Arthur Hopcraft, John Arlott and Frank Keating, should require no introduction. They and their readers could count themselves lucky that fate arranged their careers to intersect at some point with that of Best.

The first sighting is recorded by an anonymous special correspondent, covering Manchester United's home match against West Bromwich Albion on a Saturday afternoon in September 1963. The 17-year-old is making his League debut, and prompts the move that leads to the only goal. Before long he is laying on a regular stream of passes from which Bobby Charlton and Denis Law, the established greats of Matt Busby's team, add to their personal goal tally. Before the end of that first season, McIlvanney glimpses him twisting past the attempted tackles of three Liverpool defenders before finally being brought to a halt by Ron Yeats, Bill Shankly's colossus of a centre half. A couple of weeks later Todd is at Old Trafford to see United's youngsters, including Best, David Sadler, John Fitzpatrick and John Aston, play their Manchester City counterparts in the first leg of the FA Youth Cup semi-final in front of a crowd of 30,000.

Best has turned 18 by the time Todd sees him inducing "an attack of vertigo" in Eddie McCreadie, Chelsea's skilful Scottish left back, and beating Peter Bonetti with a 20-yard drive from a narrow angle on the way to a 4–0 drubbing of Tommy Docherty's gifted team; according to the historical consensus, this is the match that would turn Best's career into a headline item. Soon Barham is noting how the Irish boy can start on the right wing but is just as likely to turn up on the left, or even in the middle of the attack. The same writer is the lucky witness of the 5–1 demolition of Eusebio's Benfica in Lisbon's Stadium of Light in March 1966, the night when Best scores twice and announces himself as a talent of world class. But the praise is not unmixed: very early on, Todd spots Best's tendency to react unwisely to physical abuse, regardless of the size of his assailant. David Lacey, too, notes how Best, responsible for United's only goal in an otherwise dismal defeat away to Nottingham Forest, "celebrates" his success by giving his team mates the sort of old-fashioned look that leaves no doubt about his opinion of the quality of their performance. But a few months later Lacey is at Highbury, describing a Best goal against Arsenal in terms that could have been lifted intact from a contemporary report of one of Ronaldinho's shimmying, shimmering masterpieces.

And so it continues: the mischievous jink around the goalkeeper in the historic 1968 European Cup final victory over Benfica, the dismal sending-off in the second leg of the World Club Championship against the appalling Estudiantes de la Plata later that year, carefully recorded by Hopcraft – who then sees him, against Wolves, "avid for the ball, as he has not been all season" and "inventive in its use far beyond his form for many matches".

Now the criticisms begin to gather momentum, the occasional flawed performance beginning to rival even such a feat as his six goals scored out of United's eight in a Cup match at Northampton Town, and exposing the diminishing concentration of a man, still in his early twenties, from whom the temptations of superstardom are beginning to exact a price. "If I'd been born ugly," he tells McIlvanney, "you'd never have heard of Pelé." And soon England's football reporters are becoming amateur psychiatrists, rummaging around amid the disciplinary lapses and the increasingly frequent stories of unreliable behaviour in order to extract the evidence that will determine the extent to which Best's love of hedonistic pursuits is eroding the will to express his talent on a Saturday afternoon. Before long, indeed, Saturday afternoons are no longer sacred to the game: instead of joining the team for a match against Chelsea at Stamford Bridge he is to be found on the other side of London, holed up in the Islington flat of a well known Shakespearian actress, with half of Fleet Street's photographers camped outside.

The analyses intensify, along with the pleas – by John Samuel, the *Guardian's* sports editor, among others – for a show of understanding on the part of football's authorities towards a man whose play has brought so much artistry and entertainment to the game, and who has demonstrably been more sinned against than sinning in the matter of discipline on the pitch. "No one who has seen Best's bruised and battered body after some matches, or indeed the pictures, should be in much doubt of the provocation he has suffered," Samuel writes. And on this occasion the entreaties find a response.

But we are already into the endgame of Best's career with Manchester United. He disappears, he returns to the fold, he is confined to his digs like an errant apprentice by the new manager, Frank O'Farrell, and he gives a few more demonstrations of genius before bowing out of Old Trafford. "It is gratifying to be able to write again about Best as a footballer," Todd writes in a report of United's 4-1 win over Southampton in January 1972. "Whatever his domestic problems he showed no signs of external pressures last night . . . He was impudent and he was brilliant. He was unselfish and he was incomparable."

In Todd's words, as in those of Barham, Hopcraft, Lacey and, above all, McIlvanney, the love of Best's art and the affection for the man himself are unmistakable and unashamed. To Hopcraft, the young man's misdemeanours are "almost all of them regrettable more for their petulance and silliness than for any violence . . ." It is Arlott who, while Best's troubles are piling up, perceptively and compassionately notes that for the footballer turned celebrity, "realities must often become confused with the unknown." But finally the breach between Best and United cannot be closed, and he is on his way – first announcing that he will never play football again, then resuming his career with a variety of lesser clubs, including Stockport County, the Los Angeles Aztecs and Fulham, where Keating watches him team up with Rodney Marsh to galvanise dear old Craven Cottage, albeit briefly. "Listen, mate," Marsh tells Keating of his partnership with Best, "if only 50 per cent of what we two try together comes off, it will still be 200 per cent more than any other wanker in the league."

But now Best cannot sidestep the unwanted attention that comes with his way of life. He is arrested on a charge of stealing property from the flat of one of his girlfriends, a former Miss World, bailed and then acquitted. He crashes his car into a lamp post outside Harrods after a night at Tramp. ("Doctors believe that the cuts on Best's forehead . . . will heal and not spoil his looks," the *Guardian*'s news pages report with due solemnity.) The final indignity is to be sacked by Hibernian only a few weeks after joining them, having preferred a night of revelry with a gang of rugby fans to preparing for a match against Ayr United. Five years later, in 1984, comes the spell in Ford open prison after he is found guilty of assault and driving while drunk.

The last decade sees him at his favourite table in the Phene Arms, his Chelsea local, downing spritzers and receiving a procession of interviewers who gaze at his bloated, unshaven features in search of the shadow of the boy whose talent and beauty held the sixties in thrall and whose tales of adventures with amour and alcohol provide them with an inexhaustible source of material. A few of these writers, such as Andrew Billen and Sabine Durrant, capture the pathos without diminishing the talent.

His death, long foretold, comes on Friday, 25 November 2005, at the end of a series of bright late-autumn days such as those that so often provided a setting for the artistry of his prime. And later that day Michael Walker, the *Guardian*'s north-east football correspondent, takes up his pen to describe the simple pride he felt in having grown up close to Best's home on Belfast's Cregagh estate and in attending the same Lisnasharragh school, where the pupils of Walker's generation would ask boys from other local establishments "who their most famous ex-pupil was, so they would ask back." That an indirect memory of a man's greatness should be so vividly touching is surely the measure of a life shaped by the trajectory of Best's choice, in which he defined his own pinnacles and, when all is said and done, determined his own conclusion.

Richard Williams
September 2006

WEST BROMWICH LACK WINNING GUILE
A Special Correspondent

Manchester United: 1
West Bromwich Albion: 0

If results are all-important in the Football League —
and financial pressures seem to be taking the game well
along that road — then Manchester United could be
reasonably satisfied with their win 1-0 over West
Bromwich Albion at Old Trafford on Saturday.

United were weakened by the absence of Law and
Moir, and had to bring in Stiles at inside right and
G. Best, a 17-year-old former Irish schoolboy international, at outside right for his first league match.
Team changes forced by injury are undesirable at any
time but the disturbance of the side which has been in
such fine form seemed singularly unfortunate for this
meeting with West Bromwich, who are lying second,
behind United, in the table. In the event the absence of
Law, and to a lesser extent Moir, did not cost United
points, but it did rob the match of much of its
prospective quality.

West Bromwich, who seemed grossly flattered by
their League position, were without the guile to exploit
their advantage and in attack had not the weight to
bludgeon their way through a remorseless United
defence. With the home side suffering a similar poverty
of attacking ideas against defenders even less com-
promising in their tackling than Setters and company
the game was largely one of negative midfield mastery
by the wing halves.

Charlton alone lifted the match from the rut of
mediocrity. Throwing orthodox positional play to the
winds Charlton turned up all over the field, especially
in the second half, weaving his way through the West
Bromwich defence in an attempt to inject some fire into
the United forward line. There is no more thrilling

sight in all football than Charlton in full cry, but he is essentially a soloist and, entertaining though the attempt was, his effort to integrate the attack never really came off. Indeed it was seen how much the encouraging displays of Chisnall and Sadler this season have owed to the presence of Law. Both seemed lost without their mentor.

Young Best came in for some stern treatment by that splendid back Williams and twice sought refuge for short spells on the opposite wing where he faced Crawford, a 19-year-old, who on his first appearance in the League must have been grateful that Charlton had chosen the afternoon to go awandering. Best's football was occasionally of a high quality but he also showed his immaturity and it says much for his spirit that he twice returned to the right wing to take on Williams again who seemed intent on showing a disapproving crowd that there is no sentiment in football. Best started the move which brought the goal after 65 minutes when he directed a short pass inside to Stiles. The inside right's square pass across the penalty area found Sadler standing unmarked and as Potter despairingly advanced Sadler coolly slammed the ball past him.

In the first half Stiles beat Potter to a through ball from Charlton, but hit an upright. This apart, neither goal was ever in much danger. Howe tried hard to get the West Bromwich forwards moving but it was unrewarding work behind a line in which Foggo never caused Cantwell a moment's concern, and the three inside forwards could not shake the grip of the United half-back line. United remain unbeaten and have the return of Law and Moir to look forward to. Not even the wildest optimist in West Bromwich could draw even a crumb of such solid comfort from this match.

Manchester United: Gregg; Dunne, Cantwell, Crerand, Foulkes, Sellers, Best, Stiles, Sadler, Chisnall, Charlton.
West Bromwich Albion: Potter; Crawford, Williams, Howe, Jones, Simpson, Foggo, Cram, Readfern, Fenton, Clark.
Referee: G. W. Grundy (Grimsby).

Guardian, 16 September 1963

LAW GIVES GOALS WITH A SMILE
Tony Pawson

West Bromwich Albion: 1
Manchester United: 4

Manchester United are the most mercurial of sides but, on their day, they are altogether too good for the merely competent like Albion. Their forward play was as exciting as the names suggested it ought to be. None was more effective than Charlton, using his special talents to best advantage at centre forward.

His effortless acceleration and sudden swerve sent him gliding past his opponents as if their tackling was designed only for exercise rather than effect.

His shooting is no longer as sure and powerful as of old, but he is always threatening danger.

From the start this was a red-blooded game, with bone in the ground and beef in the play. One had only to watch Best trotting awkwardly down the left wing like a foal on ice to appreciate how difficult the conditions were if you worried about them.

Yet the play was surprisingly swift and sure, despite the problems in checking or turning. And even Best was to score the decisive goal after a delicate dribble that left Howe groping.

Only at the start did the ball seem to have a will of its own, evading the players as skilfully as if it were able to take part in the game itself, ungoverned by dull natural laws. United soon brought it firmly under control, their hard passing and quick movement ideally suited to the conditions.

They took the lead as Herd, racing clear on the right, squared the ball low into the rush of his forwards for Charlton to hook home.

But for a time the Albion wing halves sustained a fierce challenge in midfield, and it was Simpson who was quick to retaliate. Calling imperiously for a pass from Howe he hit a long shot swerving under the bar. His leap of joy outdid Gaskell's unavailing jump to save.

After the interval Law, Charlton and Herd moved with too much speed and understanding to be contained any longer. Law switching the ball to the far touchline saw Best gather it, flick it over Howe's head and calmly run it into the net.

Again the Albion defence was caught off balance by a sudden change in the point of attack leaving Herd unmarked. His shot was too hard for Potter to hold and Law swept the ball home.

Law, playing with genial good humour, was in position again to turn home Herd's pass just in time to beat the final whistle.

Albion had been beaten long before.

West Bromwich Albion: Potter; Howe, Williams, Fraser, Jones, Simpson, Clark, Fenton, Kaye, Fudge, Carter.
Manchester United: Gaskell; Dunne, Cantwell, Crerand, Foulkes, Sellers, Herd, Moore, Charlton, Law, Best.

Observer, 19 January 1964

FOR UNITED, NO GOALS ADDS UP TO A TRIUMPH
Hugh McIlvanney

Liverpool: 0
Manchester United: 0

This game will be remembered for its significance, not for its impact. Its hour-and-a-half of negative action had the positive effect of making Manchester United undisputed favourites to win the League Championship. For them a draw was something close to a triumph.

Both teams went into the match anxious to protect the profits of seven months' hard work, determined to emerge with their chances of the title undiminished. Liverpool, with two points to make up, had to play for goals. But the implications of losing a point were too serious to permit adventurousness.

The effects of the tension were cruelly exacerbated by a wind that swirled furiously and unpredictably across the field throughout the afternoon. Simultaneously buffeted by this and the challenges of frantic defenders, the forwards rarely found it possible to compose themselves for the telling shot and in the end the result accurately reflected the shared frustration.

It was particularly unfortunate for Liverpool that three of the most likely openings fell to Hunt, a player who, for all his other qualities, sometimes gives the impression that he would find difficulty in controlling the ball on a bowling green in a flat calm. Here the treacherous swerves and bounces had him labouring like a man in cricket pads. St John's industry was more conspicuous than his influence, Thompson was typically inconsistent, and Callaghan's tireless harrying was as much a defensive as an attacking factor.

Strong, as expected, was withdrawn to assist Stevenson in the middle of the field but he lacks the imagination for the job. Though the Scot went thrusting through with the forwards now and then, this weakness at the heart of the team meant that too much of Liverpool's play was harmlessly lateral.

All this was emphasised by the fact that their most dangerous weapon was Yeats's head. The huge centre half did well enough in defence too, but there he was overshadowed by Smith, who covered with devouring efficiency.

Smith's tendency to impose a physical solution on his problems frequently obscures his technical soundness. But his behaviour never threatened to mar the excellence of this performance. In fact Hughes, the new left back, was guilty of more rash tackles. Perhaps it is a partial excuse that he was exposed to the skills of Best, who gave heartening if occasional glimpses of the most devastating close control in English football.

Law began with a fine show of urgency, was obliged to abandon his total commitment to striking because of pressures behind, and found when he returned to the front running role that he could make himself felt only in isolated moments.

There was rather too much muscle in evidence for Charlton's peace of mind, and he remained peripheral. Aston was similarly subdued, although he came back with Best to help withstand the siege mounted by Liverpool in the second half.

United's most obvious hope of victory had come from Crerand, whose play in the first half hour was almost flawless. Taming the ball with thrilling ease, thinking constructively in the tightest situations, and judging his passes in the wind with an accuracy that would have done credit to the iron shots of an Arnold Palmer, he alone gave shape to that nervous early period. However, in the second half even Crerand was caught up in the necessity of saving a point. No one did more distinguished work in that struggle than Dunne at right back, whose coolly precise clearances several times averted the disaster of a goal.

Stiles, of course, was in the midst of the fight, rising from desperate interceptions to hurl abusive advice at those around him. As far as persistence went he had little advantage over Noble, who pursued Callaghan deep into the Liverpool penalty area.

A foul by Yeats on Best and an angry collision between the centre half and Law gave the game an ill-tempered start but the fears engendered by that omen were gradually allowed to subside.

When Crerand swerved inside from the right touch-line, his left-footed cross was headed down by Law in front of Sadler. But the centre forward was crowded out. Again Sadler failed to struggle through the thrashing legs as he reached for a centre by Aston. An offside decision was the centre forward's next frustration as he attempted to exploit splendid play by Crerand.

Stiles had been warned for a wild kick on Hunt but the real violence was now off the field. Behind the United goal a great space suddenly cleared in the crowd to accommodate a series of vicious fights.

In front of these unheeding spectators St John tried a brave overhead kick. Then a cross from the left was dragged ominously away from the straining Manchester defenders by the wind. Sadler was once more offside as a Best pass set him running, but Hughes, whose family have rugby traditions, dragged him down with an arm anyway.

With 40 minutes played, the United defence generously allowed St John to cross from the right and Callaghan wheeled on the ball after it had been partly cleared to deliver a powerful half-volley, which was slightly deflected before Stepney touched it over his crossbar. From the corner Yeats struck a big header but it was headed away by Stiles.

In the second half Liverpool showed more authority. Hunt had a chance almost immediately, but Dunne intervened while the forward was steadying himself. In the 57th minute a Callaghan corner gave Yeats another header and this time Stiles dropped on his haunches to take the ball on his chest.

Best skipped Stevenson and Hughes into almost cosmic confusion on the right wing, but eventually he was roughly dispossessed on the byline. A wild shot from Law almost became a good pass, but Lawrence slid out to save at Sadler's feet.

In the main the pressure was from Liverpool, and when Best inadvertently outwitted Crerand, Stevenson went clear to square to Thompson whose shot brought a difficult, grovelling save from Stepney. The goalkeeper injured himself thwarting St John, but was still fit enough to clutch a hooked shot from Hunt under his bar after yet another menacing header from Yeats.

Soon he was driving in front of Hunt to make up for a grotesque miskick by Stiles. In between Best had swerved and twisted beyond three despairing tackles only to be halted by Yeats on the edge of the box.

With only a minute or so left, however, the winger exploited the free kick that came from a foul on Law to gain a corner for his side. The time wasted meant gaining a draw and that was enough for United.

Liverpool: Lawrence; Lawler, Hughes, Smith, Yeats, Stevenson, Callaghan, Strong, St John, Hunt, Thompson.
Manchester United: Stepney; Dunne, Noble, Crerand, Foulkes, Stiles, Best, Law, Sadler, Charlton, Aston.
Referee: Mr E. T. Jennings (Stourbridge).

Observer, 26 March 1964

UNITED WIN BATTLE BETWEEN MANCHESTER YOUTHS
Eric Todd

Manchester United Youths: 4
Manchester City Youths: 1

Manchester United, showing superior ideas of finishing, beat Manchester City 4-1 in the first leg of their FA Youth Challenge Cup semi-final at Old Trafford last night, so that City face a considerable task in the second leg at Moss Side on Monday week.

A crowd of nearly 30,000 watched an entertaining and often uncompromising game and many must have seen far less worthy displays in the League. There was no lack of enthusiasm and plenty of skill, especially from the wing halves. Although City had the better of things in the first half, they just could not round off their moves. Neither Jones nor Sadler was allowed much scope, but there was some enterprising raiding by the wings and goalmouth incidents by the dozen. A rousing night, and the next argument should be no less absorbing.

City were in lively mood at the start and after Connor had headed wide Frost delivered a couple of worthy shots, one of them with an overhead kick. United survived this pressure and in their first major attack they took the lead with as good a goal as one could wish to see. Aston beat Doyle before centring low and hard into the City goalmouth and Kinsey, timing his run-in to perfection, volleyed the ball past Ogley from close range. When City retaliated, Wood headed the ball over the United crossbar and injured himself in the process. He was soon in action again, however, and keeping a close watch on Sadler.

City, inspired by two excellent wing halves, did most of the attacking, but the United defence, in which Fitzpatrick created a most favourable impression, conceded little ground. Clay won deserved applause for a clever run, during which he beat four opponents, and although he finally lost the ball, he wasted no time in getting it back again and testing Rimmer with a left-footed shot. A few minutes later Pardoe missed a good chance of equalising when he miskicked from eight yards' range. Finishing thus far had not been City's strong point whereas United were always dangerous with fewer opportunities. Eight minutes before half time Anderson centred accurately from the dead-ball line and Kinsey scored his second goal, this time with a fine header.

United were much more thorough in the second half and they should have had a penalty when Best was brought down from behind. Unfortunately for United, the referee had fallen flat near the halfway line and had only a worm's eye view of the incident and that was not good enough. In the 65th minute United were compensated. They were awarded a free kick a yard or two outside the penalty area and Kinsey completed his hat trick with a first-time shot. Two minutes afterwards Pardoe reduced the arrears, the ball hitting the underside of the crossbar and bouncing down over the line.

Five minutes from the end City's defence faltered and Sadler scored an easy fourth goal for United.

Manchester United: Rimmer; Duff, Noble, McBride, Farrar, Fitzpatrick, Anderson, Best, Sadler, Kinsey, Aston.
Manchester City: Ogley; Doyle, Wild, Clay, Wood, Burrows, Frost, Pardoe, Jones, McAlinden, Connor.
Referee: K. Dagnall (Bolton).

Guardian, 9 April 1964

MANCHESTER UNITED MAKE IT LOOK SO VERY EASY

Brian Crowther

Manchester United: 7
Aston Villa: 0

Manchester United's Celtic brigade was in rare form at Old Trafford where Aston Villa, in spite of a lively resistance, were beaten 7-0.

United's was not a triumph of patterned teamwork, but rather an inspirational victory that suited the Irish temperament and the Scottish capacity for work. Success came with a seeming ease, a deceit common to all physical artistry. Two of the goals by which United early ruined Villa's cause were gems of their kind.

The first, after 18 minutes, was a neatly placed firm header by Herd to Connelly's forceful centre from the dead ball line. The second, two minutes later, was perfect. Best drew the ball back from a defender and centred square, low, and hard to Law who timed his drive beautifully, crashing the ball into the net from nearly 20 yards – two pure moves and a peerless goal.

These were the only goals before the interval, but Law and Best, each apparently inspired and fascinated by the other's brilliance, seemed likely sources of further scoring. Best, a slippery player, goes through defences like a knife through butter without employing any such exaggerated movements as the Matthews shimmy. Like some good spin bowlers, he does not have to turn the ball much to beat his man.

For all their skill individually, United had their hands full coping with Villa in the first half. Shortly before the interval P. Dunne, a curious mixture of good and bad, was either very lucky or exceptionally alert in coping with a fierce shot by MacLeod.

Woosnam clearly was not back to full fitness, and he seemed wary of testing his right leg, which was heavily bandaged. Tindall, Hateley, and Wylie worked hard to cover up for him, but this took its toll in the second half. Villa's luck was really out for, 10 minutes from the end when United were leading 6-0, Hateley collided with United's goalkeeper, injured a leg, and was carried from the field on a stretcher.

Law scored United's third seven minutes after the interval when he got the ball from a harassed defender and drove it from 20 yards. Sidebottom could only help it into the net. Connelly made it 4-0 five minutes later when the ball returned to him off the crossbar during a mix-up in the Villa goalmouth, and Law scored his third and United's fifth when he took a pass from Crerand, sidestepped the diving goalkeeper, and shot the ball home.

Herd, who with Crerand had contributed much to the good work of the Scottish faction, scored with an unstoppable shot when the ball ran free from Pountney's tackle on Law. Villa, because desperation made them try harder, were more effective when Hateley left the field, and P. Dunne did well to save twice from Wylie.

But almost on time, Law scored his fourth goal with a header to Stiles's bouncing centre. Like the victory, it was accomplished professionally yet casually.

Manchester United: Dunne (P.); Brennan, Dunne (A.), Crerand, Foulkes, Sellers, Connelly, Stiles, Herd, Law, Best.
Aston Villa: Sidebottom; Wright, Aitken, Tyndall, Sleeuwenhoek, Pountney, MacLeod, Woosnam, Hateley, Wylie, Burrows.
Referee: P. Baldwin (Middlesbrough).

Guardian, 26 October 1964

TRIUMPH OF MANCHESTER UNITED
From a Correspondent

Borussia Dortmund: 1
Manchester United: 6

Manchester United gave their most convincing and rewarding performance on the Continent since their two seasons in the European Cup competition of seven and eight years ago when they beat Borussia Dortmund 6-1 here tonight in the first leg of their Inter City Fairs Cup second round match.

Only a fortnight ago Borussia were top of the German National League, yet they were astonishingly outclassed at times by United. Charlton scored three fine goals and the youthful Best delighted even the Germans in the 25,000 crowd with his brilliant footwork.

United's opening was for a moment reminiscent of their last game in European competition when they were humiliated and beaten 3-0 by Sporting Club of Portugal in the Cup Winners' Cup last season. One or two misplaced passes and strong pressure from Borussia forced United onto the defensive. Law had to come back and help out, clearing a shot from Beyer over his own goal.

This phase lasted a mere five minutes. Stiles left his colleagues in defence and joined in the first of many devastating raids. Charlton twice went close and in the 12th minute Herd brought United the lead. Law fastened on to a rebounding shot, headed the ball into the air, trapped it neatly, and sent Herd darting through. United's centre forward beat Wessel with one of his low drives that have been a feature of his success in recent matches.

The goal immediately made United confident and they played with the sort of assurance that is usually the prerogative of home teams in this competition.

Charlton, Best, and Law began to beat their opponents with an ease and grace that was delightful. It was quite in keeping with the play that Charlton increased the lead by finishing a strong run with a shot to match it. The ball crashed into goal off the underside of the crossbar, putting United two goals up in the first half hour.

A party of British servicemen began to chant "Easy." But Borussia were still prepared to make a fight of it and twice Dunne, the goalkeeper, had to leap brilliantly to keep the lead for United. He did well to thwart Konietzka, who was the Germans' best marksman.

Five minutes after the interval Best brought United a commanding lead of 3-0. He wormed his way through the Borussia defence and calmly steered the ball past Wessel. Two German spectators had been saying how much they admired this young Irishman. Now they turned to the press box, confirming not just their command of English but their judgement in saying: "Best is best."

Certainly he was having a remarkable game. United faltered slightly in the 52nd minute when Crerand was a little late in to a tackle on Kurrat. The referee had no hesitation in awarding a penalty which was success-fully taken by Kurrat. Perhaps United had memories of their first leg against Borussia Dortmund in the European Cup of 1956 when they slumped at Moss Side from a lead of 3-0 to 3-2.

Best, though, showed no sign of panic and again worked his way through almost the entire German defence. The rest of the forward line responded so successfully that the Germans fell away badly. Borussia played as if they were over conscious of their last two defeats in the League, which translated them from leaders to sixth.

By the end, United were toying with them. Law rose high in heading a goal in the 77th minute from Best's centre. Two minutes later Charlton took a pass from

Law and scored United's fifth goal. Just before the end he scored his third with another powerfully hit shot.

United lost a lead of three goals in the Cup Winners' Cup in Portugal last season but one cannot see them failing with this advantage against Borussia at Old Trafford in the second leg on 2 December.

Borussia Dortmund: Wessel: Cyliax, Reffer, Kurrat, Paul, Sturn, Yosan, Brungs, Beyer, Konietzka, Emmereich.
Manchester United: Dunne (P.); Brennan, Dunne (A.), Crerand, Foulkes, Stiles, Connelly, Charlton, Herd, Law, Best.
Referee: Rigato (Italy).

Guardian, 12 November 1964

CHELSEA RELEGATED TO SECOND FIDDLE
Eric Todd

Manchester United: 4
Chelsea: 0

Manchester United who, according to pernickety observers, "do not always press home their advantage," beat Chelsea 4-0 at Old Trafford on Saturday. Thus they completed the double over the League leaders, and brought their harvest of goals to nine in two consecutive matches. So much for negligence!

Roget's Thesaurus itself stands in danger of being denuded of adequate adjectives with which to describe this United side, whose members delight in blasting criticism sky high. Let it be whispered that the backs are too slow and inexperienced, and Brennan and A. Dunne excel themselves as they did on Saturday. Let it be suggested that Crerand's passes are inconsistent, and he dominates the whole proceedings. And if the slightest hint be dropped that when Law is comparatively subdued United's attack is no more than ordinary, study the reactions of Herd, Best, Connelly, and Charlton. United can make fools of everyone, except themselves.

All of which is designed to dispel a widespread belief that United are a one-man team. There was a time, perhaps, when Law helped to create that illusion, but not any more. There is nothing stereotyped about United's play. They are versatile and have mastered the difficult art of improvisation. The numbers on their shirts are for identification only – where identification is needed. Every man has learned at least one other part, so that if someone forgets his words, so to say, there is no waiting for the prompter. I would not say yet that United are a great side, but greatness is on the very near horizon.

Chelsea never had a hope of saving the day, yet they played some stylish football and at no time did they resort to that peevish behaviour that so often accompanies frustration. Not often has defeat received such chivalrous acknowledgement, and even the partisan colony at the Stretford end registered its appreciation of Chelsea's overall performance. It was defeat with dignity.

Two main factors encompassed Chelsea's downfall. The first was United's sudden lead. The second was that Crerand throughout dictated the tempo at which he wished his orchestra to play – *andante ma non troppo*. Chelsea, I think, prefer *allegro vivace*. But Venables lacked the persuasive control of Crerand, and his own players frequently found themselves a bar or two behind or else out of tune.

Furthermore, Chelsea were unexpectedly slow in recovery and retaliation. Once or twice their forwards combined quite splendidly, but, when they retreated, they and their backs seemed concerned more with consolidating their defences than with breaking out again. The result was that most of the pressure was on the Chelsea goal, and Bonetti, who made some superb saves, was grossly overworked. Chelsea's bright young men – and they are just that – were given a salutary lesson in tactics, and it will do them no harm.

The game was three minutes old when Best, having induced an attack of vertigo on McCreadie, drove the ball over Bonetti's head from a narrow angle of 20 yards out, a brilliant effort. Twenty minutes afterwards Stiles and Crerand confounded the Chelsea defenders and helped Herd to score United's second goal. Not until the last minute of the first half did Chelsea muster a worthwhile attack, and then Bridges, Murray, Hollins, and Graham, its manufacturers, had reason to look sad when Tambling headed the ball over the crossbar.

Early in the second half Herd turned the ball past Bonetti after a hard centre by the irrepressible Best who, 15 minutes from the end, gave the ball to Law and he in turn left Mortimer sitting on the ground before driving the ball home. Venables and Bridges never relaxed their efforts to reduce the leeway, but United gave Chelsea nothing except hospitality and a warning that there is as much space available for the FA Challenge Cup and the Football League Championship Cup in the boardroom at Old Trafford as there is in that at Stamford Bridge – and Elland Road, too, for that matter.

Manchester United: Dunne (P.); Brennan, Dunne (A.), Crerand, Foulkes, Stiles, Connelly, Charlton, Herd, Law, Best.
Chelsea: Bonetti; Hinton, McCreadie, Hollins, Mortimer, Harris, Murray, Graham, Bridges, Venables, Tambling.
Referee: G. McCabe (Sheffield).

Guardian, 15 March 1965

MANCHESTER UNITED SHOW QUALITY OF CHAMPIONS
Albert Barham

Birmingham City: 2
Manchester United: 4

In this crucial period of the struggle for the Football League Championship, experience, power and craft are telling. So it was at St Andrews yesterday, where Manchester United, stung at being a goal down to Birmingham City, struck back to equalise within a minute and to go two up within 12 minutes. Here, indeed, was the stuff of which champions are made. Victory by 4–2 was just.

Yet Birmingham, destined to play in the Second Division next season, played with tremendous fire and verve, though hampered by an injured player – Fraser's thigh was swathed in strapping after a knock early in the game. Such determination made for a match that, in spite of the biting wind and the flurries of snow and rain, never lacked excitement, enthusiasm, or purpose.

United stormed into the lead with a goal as early as the 13th minute, when the shaggy head of Best glided from behind the back of Foster to flick Connelly's clever centre into the net. Best stole through this game, a ghostly figure materialising on the right wing, then on the left, or appearing in the centre, as he did on this occasion, and once again, just after the hour, to signal the tremendous revival, and to demonstrate United's power of recovery, with the second goal.

In between, City had their moments, with Thwaites active on one wing, and Jackson furtively sending over centres on the other. These two wing forwards contrived Birmingham's first goal, Thwaites bringing the scores level in the 27th minute, from Jackson's pass. And, while United were missing opportunities regularly, City had their lapses, too. Beard twice muffed chances he would give his eye-teeth to have again.

Hennessey and Foster were the power in a City side who for one minute seemed to have the edge over United. It was as brief as that, for City went ahead in the 62nd minute, through Bowden. He lurked on the edge of the penalty area, and, with a delicate flick, pushed another pass from Thwaites past P. Dunne. But from that moment of adversity came forth the strength of United.

They were level again in a minute, through Best, a goal ahead two minutes later, through Charlton and, finally, 15 minutes from time, Cantwell, socks rolled down to the ankles with the effort of it all, rose high to nod in the fourth goal. Such excitement drew swarms of young supporters cavorting over the pitch, but a stern warning over the loudspeaker system that the referee would stop the match if they did not desist soon sent them back.

Even then, the excitement was not at its end, for Foster bounced a ball warningly off the United cross-bar. It was a reminder to United that they could not relax, even when everything seemed assured. Their supporters were confident. They were in great voice, assuring St Andrews and the surrounding city, to a tune borrowed from Anfield, "We'll win the League." Quite probably United will.

Guardian, 20 April 1965

BENFICA ARE DESTROYED BY UNITED'S FURY
Albert Barham

Benfica: 1
Manchester United: 5
(*Manchester United win 8-3 on aggregate*)

Manchester United move on once again to the semi-finals of the European Cup. Commandingly imperiously, they crushed the Eagles of Benfica here tonight with as magnificent a display of attacking football as one has ever seen. Three goals came in 15 minutes, two from that elusive genius Best, another from Connelly, and finally, in the dying minutes, Crerand and Charlton ground all the hope out of Benfica.

What a mockery it all made of the theory that a team has to be defensive away from home; United came to Lisbon last night to prove themselves, as their manager, Mr M. Busby, said. One does not merely tempt fate in asking who can stop them now. If they can reproduce the form they showed tonight they will be without doubt the finest club side in Europe.

And how United earned all the praise they will receive! Here we saw the greatness of teamwork and team spirit, spiced with skill to match. Benfica had no answer, and their frustrated supporters at the end hurled cushions in disgust. However there was only one moment of ugliness when United's trainer, J. Crompton, was involved in a scuffle in attempting to shield his players as they left the pitch.

This, of course, was the match of the season for United and the lead of one goal United had from Old Trafford and the glowing reports of the fine attacking football brought in the crowds. 70,000 packed this beautiful ground. The fingers of light topped by the winged eagles of Benfica flooded the scene. Not surprisingly this stadium is called the Stadium of Light. But who among this vast crowd could have thought

United would score three goals here in the first 15 minutes.

What a shock it was for Benfica. Pinto fouled Charlton after six minutes. Dunne took the kick far out on the left and up rose Best high above a mass of Benfica shirts to head United's first goal this evening. It left the crowd silent in disbelief. Mr Busby, United's manager, had said they would attack when they could from their 4-4-2 formation, and attack they did.

In the long preliminaries which preceded this match Eusebio was presented with the award as the European footballer of the year. With all due regard to Eusebio it was not his night. It was, indeed, United's in every phase of the game from the way they marshalled their defences to the way they struck suddenly in attack. Never have Benfica been so confounded as by the impishness of such players as Best, the strength of Charlton, and the tremendous support both received from the half-back line.

Only once in the first 20 minutes was there a hint as at Old Trafford, of the panther-eyed moves of Eusebio. What a tribute to United and to their attack this was. In the 12th minute they went further ahead. A long clearance was headed back to Best from Herd, and Best took the ball in his stride, raced forward a dozen steps, and smashed the ball under Pereira's falling body. And a third followed four minutes later. Best had a foot in that, too. But it was Connelly who hammered his return pass into the goal.

Benfica's manager brought in Silva, who has been injured, to take the place of Nelson, but after these three quick goals from United there was little for some time from the Benfica forward line. The great question was whether they would recover some of their poise, but it is an awful task to pull back four goals, even for a team like Benfica. Yet there was one warning after 30 minutes when Eusebio hit the foot of a United post with a free kick taken after he had been hacked down by Stiles.

Again it was Connelly who bemused Cavem with his swift change of direction and from that pass in the closing minutes of the first half Pereira leapt to his left to palm away one of the shots for which Charlton is known the world over. But as this match pulsed with excitement on into the second half there was a resurgence of spirit from Benfica, for the greatness of a team can be measured by its power of recovery. But it was all too short and too often Benfica were left with only a hopeful long shot to smash against the wall of United defenders. There was, however, a moment of disappointment for United in the 52nd minute as Brennan, attempting to keep the ball from Eusebio, hooked it too far to the right of Gregg and it rolled into his own net.

There was almost another mishap on the hour when a back pass from Brennan fell too short of Gregg who eventually won a race for the ball with Torres. But gradually United regained control and Charlton, Best, Connelly and Herd worked together splendidly only for Herd, rather too carefree, to stab the ball wide.

Then it was Law's turn to send Pereira flying to tip away a fierce shot. Again Best was the provider and this was one of the moves which made the match one to savour. Long will it remain in the memory, all the more so because of United's two final goals, the fourth coming 10 minutes from time as Crerand pounced on to a perfectly timed pass which opened up Benfica's defence from Law and the fifth seconds from time as Charlton waltzed through the defence and delayed his shot with almost a touch of insolence.

Benfica: Costa Pereira; Cavem, Germano, Cruz, Pinto, Coluna, Augusto Silva, Eusebio, Torres, Jose Augusto, Simoes.
Manchester United: Gregg; Brennan, Dunne, Crerand, Foulkes, Stiles, Best, Law, Charlton, Herd, Connelly.

Guardian, 10 March 1966

UBIQUITOUS BEST MATCHES ST JOHN GOAL FOR GOAL
Eric Todd

Manchester United: 2
Liverpool: 2

Honours were even and honour was satisfied on
Saturday at Old Trafford where Manchester United,
the heirs-presumptive – heirs-apparent more like – to
the Football League Championship throne, drew 2-2
with Liverpool, its present tenants. A well-behaved
crowd of 62,500 made a handsome contribution to the
afternoon's enjoyment.

The fact that both sides were led up the garden path,
so to say, probably had the biggest single influence on
the occasion. United were mistaken if they thought
that Liverpool might not have recovered from their
recent drubbing against Ajax in Amsterdam. Liverpool
quickly were made to realise that United were neither
weakened nor embarrassed by the absence of Law and
Stiles because of injury and sickness.

It is not easy to imagine circumstances in which
"weakened" may be attributed to United, saving a
visitation by bubonic plague. They are not invulner-
able, nor are they immune against mortal frailty, but
they have a remarkable team spirit and they keep on
exhibiting precocious young men when the need arises.
Ryan had a satisfactory first senior game of the season,
and Sadler and Noble surely have made their places
secure. And, of course, United have Best.

On Saturday Best combined his own duties with
those usually carried out by Law and Stiles. Once or
twice he spoke to Stepney as if asking that admirable
goalkeeper if he would like a few minutes' break. Best's
ubiquity did not upset United's rhythm, and it testified
to his skill and ability to read the game, as well as to the
common sense of his colleagues, that United frequently

created the illusion of having more men on the field than allowed by the laws. Seldom have I seen a comparable example of perpetual and destructive motion.

Best seemingly has the strength of 10 yet sadly his heart is not always pure. He should try and tolerate fouling by lesser players and eschew reprisals. Certainly he should not pick on opponents bigger than himself – someone like Yeats, for example, whom he once flattened effectively and quite illegally. Best had his name taken.

Not necessarily because of what he did to Yeats, whom he tormented all the afternoon. Best was the local hero, although the usually partisan Stretford end admired and applauded the magnificent efforts of Milne and St John. Nearly all Liverpool's raids had their origin in the busy little Milne, and nearly all were carried out by St John, who deserved better support than in fact he received, particularly from Strong and Hunt. Stevenson, too, had a fine match, though he had his name taken when he fouled Ryan.

St John gave Liverpool the lead after 13 minutes when Sadler for once was confounded by a superb through pass by Milne. Within two minutes Herd sent Best away and Best's shot with his left foot was a winner all the way. In the 28th minute Yeats tripped Ryan and Best's successful penalty kick nearly broke the crossbar, the net, and Lawrence's heart. Just before half time St John cleverly scored his second goal after a corner.

In an equally rousing second half Stepney saved brilliantly from Thompson and Strong; Yeats thwarted (cleanly) Herd ten yards out; and United, I thought, should have been awarded a second penalty when Strong fouled Ryan. Yeats was the first to shake Best by the hand when it was all over. Yeats, like Dave Ewing yesteryear, is massive and uncompromising, but happily he is not unacquainted with chivalry.

Manchester United: Stepney; Brennan, Noble, Crerand, Sadler, Dunne (A.), Best, Ryan, Charlton, Herd, Aston. Sub: Anderson.
Liverpool: Lawrence; Lawler, Milne, Smith, Yeats, Stevenson, Callaghan, Hunt, St John, Strong, Thompson.
Referee: W. Crossley (Lancaster).

Guardian, 12 December 1966

BAN ON LAW SAPS UNITED'S SPIRIT
David Lacey

Nottingham Forest: 3
Manchester United: 1

Manchester United broke another attendance record at Nottingham on Saturday but for an hour they had little heart for the occasion. The six-week suspension on Law had subdued the side as a whole and by the time Best, with a goal which he alone could have scored, had reminded them of their high calling Forest were leading 3-0 and the game was beyond redemption. United lost 3-1, only their second defeat of the season.

Poor Law; he dragged his heels as he led United on to the field and looked as though he dreaded the game's start, let alone its end. There was none of the old fire about his play and, having gone through the motions for 90 minutes, he walked off with head bowed. Few would quarrel with the length of Law's suspension but it was a pity that the wretched business should have coincided with a fixture which usually produces a close contest and a sharp contrast in attacking styles.

On Saturday, however, most of the excitement and the larger part of the skill came from Nottingham while United, for all Charlton's exhortation, merely muddled along disconsolately. With a melancholy Law outnumbered in front of goal – two men always went up with him for the high balls – and no Stiles to inject some spirit into their play they were a poor match for a Forest side right on form.

These big matches at the City Ground simmer with tension; on Saturday the gates were closed on 49,964 people, among them a child of three who got lost halfway through the afternoon. The old record at Nottingham was 47,654 in October 1957, when the visitors were a rather different Manchester United.

Most of Saturday's crowd went home happy, for Forest are playing as well now as they will probably do all season. They have four or five players whose speed and sense of purpose once the ball is at their feet will upset the best of defences. On Saturday they set out to outpace and outflank their opponents and it was a credit to their fitness that they were running as hard at the end as at the start.

But the absence of Stiles was more directly responsible for United's defeat. Fitzpatrick, his deputy, was twice caught on the turn and twice Baker scored. The first time, in the 26th minute, Newton lobbed the ball forward and Baker ran through to catch Stepney out of goal with a header which sailed in under the bar; on the second occasion, five minutes before the interval, the ball sped from Newton to Wignall and past Fitzpatrick to Baker, who again scored emphatically. Grummitt meantime had saved superbly from Best and Charlton, and when Wignall scored a third after 59 minutes the game seemed won and lost.

Then Best showed Newton the ball twice, swerved past him and scored with an impudent shot which swung in by the near post. Best glared at his colleagues, daring them to congratulate him, and Forest, nervous now, seemed to be mindful of the way Best had tormented the Scots in Belfast – but there were no more goals.

Nottingham Forest: Grummitt; Hindley, Winfield, Hennessey, McKinlay, Newton, Lyons, Barnwell, Baker, Wignall, Moore.
Manchester United: Stepney; Kopel, Burns, Crerand, Sadler, Fitzpatrick, Best, Kidd, Law, Charlton, Aston.

Guardian, 30 October 1967

BEST'S GENIUS CONFOUNDS ARSENAL AT HIGHBURY
David Lacey

Arsenal: 0
Manchester United: 2

What should have been one of Manchester United's hardest games of the season turned out to be one of their easiest victories. Arsenal, lacking Ure, and with Neill not fully fit, were ill equipped to deal with Best, a point he emphasised in the second half with a goal of rare audacity and skill. Charlton's absence seemed utterly irrelevant, as indeed did Arsenal's unbeaten home run of 27 League and Cup games. More pertinently perhaps, they have yet to win a First Division game this year.

The match could have given Arsenal a boost of confidence for what will surely be the club's most important fortnight of the season so far – the League Cup final against Leeds United at Wembley on Saturday, followed by their FA Cup fifth round tie against Birmingham City at Highbury a week later, but it only served to confirm any lingering doubts about the present side's lack of ability at the highest level.

There were moments when it seemed that Arsenal's ingenuous style, based on everybody's willingness to run, challenge and make something out of the most unlikely situations, would bring rewards that their lack of skill denied them. Early in the game, for instance,

Simpson headed the ball to Armstrong and met the
return with a soaring volley that might have made all
the difference to the outcome had it gone a foot lower.
Just before half time Gould and Sammels went equally
close but this was the sum of Arsenal's attacking threat;
the rest of the time Graham and Gould were stifled by
Sadler and Stiles.

Manchester United's performance was a masterpiece
of controlled pace underlying the skill and ingenuity
which make them what they are. An hour of aggression
based on depth in defence and tenacity in midfield was
followed by a gentle run-down in the last 30 minutes,
when, with the match safe, wind and limb were
preserved for Gornik on Wednesday.

The cold, and possibly the prospect of a huge crowd,
kept the attendance down to 47,000 but those who
stayed away missed a great deal. Even without
Charlton, and playing at two-thirds pace, Manchester
United are still worth watching. Law, channelling his
efforts into a narrow strip of territory along the halfway line, had one of his better games. Time and again
he, Fitzpatrick, or the assured Crerand would frustrate
the efforts of McLintock, Armstrong and Sammels to
create some kind of cohesive movement in the
Manchester half. Law performed this type of limited but
effective role for the Rest of the World against England
in the FA Centenary match at Wembley in 1963; from
all accounts Scotland needed a similar feat on Saturday.

Inevitably Best stole the show. Last week his
boutique business won a £15,000 mail order contract
and Arsenal were unlucky enough to be first in line for
the celebration. He stayed upfield and poor Storey was
given Ure's job of shadowing him; as the game wore on
it became more a case of Best marking Storey. After 23
minutes they both went for a long clearance from
Stepney, which landed some way out on the right wing.
It was not immediately clear what happened next. Best
was on Storey's outside, and suddenly the ball came

flying back towards the far corner of the Arsenal goal. Furnell, taken by surprise, could not get to it. An own-goal, it transpired, although at the time one quite believed that Best had hooked the ball in from an impossible angle.

Ten minutes after the interval, however, he scored a goal that brooked no argument. Kidd centred from the left, Law met the ball near the penalty spot, and nodded it down to Best's feet. With the Arsenal defence massed in front of him Best dummied to the right, swerved inwards, turned round, took the ball two paces through a gap that he had opened up to his left and hit it into the top right hand corner of the net.

The rest of the game was played out in stunned silence on the part of the Arsenal supporters, punctuated at intervals by the squeals of those young Manchester supporters who see Best as a Beatle in football boots.

Arsenal: Furnell; Storey, McNab, McLintock, Neill, Simpson, Jenkins, Gould, Graham, Sammels, Armstrong.
Manchester United: Stepney; Dunne, Burns, Crerand, Sadler, Stiles, Best, Kidd, Fitzpatrick, Law, Aston.
Referee: D. J. Lyden (Birmingham).

Guardian, 26 February 1968

UNITED BEATEN BY SPEED
Arthur Hopcraft

Manchester United: 1
Liverpool: 2

Manchester's goal, scored inside three minutes with all the explosiveness and flair that Charlton and Best can bring to an attacking move conjured out of innocuousness, promised one of United's more inventive, dominating performances.

But just as happened against Manchester City 10 days before, it was United's brittle uncertainty in defence when confronted with unrelenting speed and power which proved the more important factor.

Liverpool's strong, hurrying forwards do not deal much in cunning or surprise; they shredded this Manchester defence by sheer insistence.

The result at this vital stage of an intriguing season must bring United's chance of eventual success into the most serious question. The kind of mistakes made by the defenders close to their own goal were the most basic ones: failure to collect the ball cleanly, indecision in going for interceptions, misjudgement in antici- pating colleagues' movements.

Both of Liverpool's goals were helped by inade- quacies like these. Earlier in the season it had been United's sure method in defence which contributed greatly to their 2-1 win at Anfield.

Best's goal had the pace, the accuracy, the thrilling sense of inevitability that characterised United's play at its finest.

Charlton, having been penalised for obstructing Yeats close to the halfway line, was astonished to find the centre half's free kick hit weakly along the ground straight to his feet. Charlton paused long enough to let Best begin his run and then hit a long, dipping pass into his stride.

The ball spun as it dropped between Best and Hughes, rushing on him, and then Best was running free with it, leaving Hughes sliding on his back. Lawrence dutifully advanced with an intimidating look, and Best struck the ball hard past him, right-footed and on the move.

Three minutes later Charlton, darting forward as the ball broke loose just outside the Liverpool penalty area, sent in a ferocious shot which Lawrence pushed round the post.

Such a beginning could be expected to impose a wary caution on most sides. But Liverpool have never had a negative approach to the game under Mr Shankly, and soon Yeats was leaping adventurously about Manchester's goal area. He headed the ball against the far post. Sadler and Dunne watched, rooted, as the ball came back into play, Lawler tried to get a foot to it and failed, and then Yeats's lunge put it into the net.

That anxiety in front of Manchester's goal was never to be expunged from the defence. In the 17th minute Crerand lost the ball to St John close to his own penalty area, Hateley managed to nudge it away from Sadler and Hunt, chasing in from the left, was barely challenged in 15 yards before he shot past Stepney.

Neither the pace nor the excitement ever diminished. Mostly United were going forward; Crerand and Charlton not often retiring further back than the half-way line, and both of them prompting Best, Herd and Gowling repeatedly.

Lawrence was worked as he seldom is behind Liverpool's astute and stern defenders. He saved bravely at Herd's feet, pushed one of Best's crosses from the byline smartly round the near post, then snatched the ball again from Herd to prevent a shot on the half volley.

Immediately before the interval Best slid the ball in front of Gowling just inside the penalty area, and Lawrence smacked the strong shot decisively away.

Gowling, a 19-year-old Manchester University economics student, who has been greatly praised locally, was playing his first League match at Old Trafford. He won a lot of applause. He is a courageous, bold forward more than a clever one; far from elegant but with a strength in his running and his shooting.

But Gowling's inexperience in the company of a defence like Liverpool's was glaring and seriously hampering. Charlton and Crerand repeatedly placed their passes adroitly where Law used to fasten fiercely on them and astonish goalkeepers. But neither Herd nor Gowling has anything like that killing sharpness.

Pressing so urgently in attack, United were bound to leave their defence stretched in frailty. Stepney was severely tested by Hunt, St John, Strong and Hughes.

But the most important save of the day was Lawrence's 15 minutes from the end, when it appeared that United must score. Crerand chipped a free kick over the defensive wall and Best shot on the run. Lawrence dived for the far post and held the ball with both hands.

Manchester United: Stepney; Dunne, Burns, Crerand, Sadler, Fitzpatrick, Best, Gowling, Charlton, Herd, Aston.
Liverpool: Lawrence; Lawler, Hughes, Ross, Yeats, Strong, Callaghan, Hunt, Hateley, St John, Thompson.

Observer, 7 April 1968

UNITED OVERWHELM BENFICA IN EXTRA TIME BURST
Albert Barham

Manchester United: 4
Benfica: 1

At last the European Cup comes to England from Manchester United's night of triumph at Wembley last night. They won just as they promised they would, not so much for themselves as for their manager, Matt Busby. Thus 11 years of trial and tragedy, effort and frustration, culminated in this great victory when it seemed again as in the semi-final in Madrid, that the cards were beginning to stack against them. What a victory it was. In seven minutes of extra time Benfica were crushed by three goals. These three came at a time when all the power and grace of Benfica's forward line – every man an international – had clawed their way back with a goal 10 minutes from time by Graca to equalise that of Bobby Charlton 27 minutes earlier.

What finer player could there be to score United's first goal than United's captain, Bobby Charlton – his first goal in European Cup football since that against Benfica in the Stadium of Light two years ago. He also scored the final goal last night, and who better? In between was a goal taken as coolly as on the practice pitch by Best, and one from Kidd to celebrate his 19th birthday.

But, goals apart, this was again a triumph of team work and spirit. Every player gave his all, from Stepney, who three times was United's saviour against the powerful shooting of Eusebio, to Foulkes, who has missed only three of United's matches in their 11 long years of waiting for this supreme moment. And there was, too, the covering of the backs, the prompting of Crerand, Aston enjoying himself on the wing and Best, so often cruelly hacked down in full flight.

This indeed was a match to remember. Though it started slowly, with a tension one could expect with the rewards so great, it was attacking in every sense of the word. Once the first flush of nervous tension had been relieved, the match blossomed. The fuse was lit by Charlton's first goal. Yet it was a game which could easily have been lost by United between the 80th and the 90th minutes. For then one saw the greatness of Eusebio and the rest of this Portugal forward line. It was then that United's defence creaked, with Eusebio the one man to exploit it. But three goals between the third and 10th minutes of extra time extinguished the spark. In 10 minutes Benfica went from a team in command to a team in defeat – and they knew it.

One thing Benfica knew was that they had to stop Best. Cruz was detailed as the chief hatchet man. At least half a dozen times in the first half Best was hurled to the turf. It was crude, perhaps; it certainly was effective. And for another foul on Best, Humberto had his name taken. But, for all the free kicks which were conceded by Benfica just outside the penalty area from these infringements, United could not capitalise. The rear four men of Benfica combine so well, and their power is shown by the fact that, up until the final, they had conceded only two goals.

For so long it had seemed that this match would be a stalemate. Each side knew so much about the other from previous encounters. United had, last night, six of the side who plucked the feathers from the tail of the Eagles of Lisbon in that 5-1 triumph two years ago. But the second half blossomed into an exciting encounter. And who could be neutral on a night like this.

Aston was enjoying himself on the left wing. As the second half opened he sent in one shot which Henrique failed to hold with his hands, but smothered with his body. Moments later, Aston crashed in another shot. But the real drama was reserved for Bobby Charlton. His goal in the 53rd minute set the game aflame and the crowd almost hysterical with delight.

A move developed down the left. Over came Sadler's cross-field pass; up went Bobby Charlton to glide the ball, with his head, into the far corner of the net. It was the first goal Bobby Charlton has scored in a European Cup tie since that memorable night in Lisbon two years ago. Last night's goal was just as brilliantly taken, but this time it was more crucial.

But this Benfica side are vastly experienced in European Cup football. And in finals, too. This was their fifth final, and nine minutes from the end, all their experience showed. They drew level with a goal by Graca. Augusto sent over the ball, Torres nodded it down, and Eusebio, full of guile, deceived the defence by going away and taking the defence with him. It opened up the gap for Graca who, with only a narrow angle of the goal to aim at, shot and scored.

United's defence, which had held the twin threat of Eusebio and Torres so well, began to creak. And Eusebio, one of the finest forwards in Europe, was just the man to exploit it. Twice he burst through in the closing minutes and twice Stepney saved his shots.

No more dramatic opening to extra time could be imagined. United swept forward and twice in two minutes they scored. In the third minute, Stepney's clearance was headed on by Kidd to Best. And here was Best seen at his most brilliant. He took the ball round the defenders, and round the goalkeeper too, before popping it into the net.

Then it was Kidd's turn. This came in the fifth minute. Sadler had a part in that goal. The first attempt at a header was beaten out by Henrique but back it came for Kidd to head in. And United were not finished. One shot bounced on the bar before, in the 10th minute, Bobby Charlton scored again, and the creator of this goal was Kidd. It was Kidd's pass which Charlton turned into the net to complete the discomfiture of Benfica.

Manchester United: Stepney; Brennan, Dunne, Crerand, Foulkes, Stiles, Best, Kidd, Charlton, Sadler, Aston.
Benfica: Henriques; Adolfo, Humberto, Jacinto, Cruz, Graca, Coluna, Augusto, Torres, Eusebio, Simoes.
Referee: C. Lo Bello (Italy)

Guardian, 30 May 1968

UNITED PAY PRICE OF BUENOS AIRES
Arthur Hopcraft

Manchester United: 0
Arsenal: 0

Midway through the second half, which was wretchedly ill-natured and profligate with error, a loudspeaker announcement warned the crowd that if any more rubbish was thrown at the Arsenal goalkeeper the referee would abandon the match.

It is fair to wonder whether either the spectators, or the players, would have been greatly offended if he had done so. Certainly both sides looked relieved to be released at the end, shaking hands and heads in such a doleful way as to give a distinct impression of shame-faced commiseration.

The first half was graced on occasion by snatches of Charlton's invention, Crerand's measured meticulous-ness, Gould's opportunism. But it was marked most memorably by Law's sad inability to take the kind of scoring chances that made his reputation and by a mixture of surliness and selfishness on the part of Best which all but destroyed his game.

Both crowd and referee made emphatic comments on that shabby second half. It opened in raggedness and ended in a crude incoherence, and it will stay in the memory a good deal longer than one could wish.

The experience in Buenos Aires against Estudiantes seems to have been more lastingly souring than was expected. The side looked morally diminished, as well as physically tired.

At least the match started brightly enough. Charlton back-heeled Crerand's free kick neatly in front of Law, only for Law to volley, too hurriedly, over the bar.

Shortly afterwards Morgan matched Charlton's accuracy with a sharp cross from his wing and Best headed over. Then Storey had to kick off his goal line, with his goalkeeper hopelessly lost out in the penalty area.

But these startling moments were not a build-up; they were merely disjointed incidents which made bearable an increasingly drab first half.

In all this half, Best, admittedly harshly treated, as always, by defenders galvanised into desperate anxiety every time he touched the ball, could not find the pace, or the persistence, that can make him the country's most damaging forward.

He had one shot deflected barely wide of the foot of a post; but twice his hugging of the ball, on a day when his loss of touch made it essential that he should release it quickly, allowed Simpson to rob him and create dangerous situations for Manchester's defence. On the second occasion Simpson was only a foot or so wide with his shot.

Arsenal's attacks were neither frequent nor imaginative, although Gould and Sammels both showed themselves capable of turning any loss of concentration by Manchester's defenders into scoring chances. Two of the best saves of the day were made by Stepney, once holding a shot from Sammels on the ground, then palming away a fiercely swerving shot from the same forward.

Charlton's calm in that disorderly second half was a thing of impressive dignity, but even he became infected with the carelessness which marked so much of both sides' work.

Close to the end, Charlton found himself with the ball at his feet and with Best and Morgan unhindered to left and right. He mishit his pass dead ahead – and held his right forefinger to his temple in self-disgust.

Manchester United: Stepney; Dunne, Burns, Crerand, Foulkes, Stiles, Morgan, Fitzpatrick, Charlton, Law, Best.
Arsenal: Wilson; Storey, McNab, McLintock, Neill, Simpson, Radford, Sammels, Gould, Court, Jenkins.

A GAME MORE OF A BORE THAN A DISGRACE
Arthur Hopcraft

Estudiantes de la Plata, in winning the World Club Championship, stayed faithful to the end to the antic gracelessness of the event. Their abrupt, offhand exit from London Airport on Thursday night, dismissing without hint of apology the matches arranged for this week against Arsenal and Birmingham, was an entirely appropriate finale: a collective gesture at England of the obscene kind that got Nobby Stiles ordered from the field in Buenos Aires.

The Argentinians' absence from Highbury tomorrow night and from St Andrews on Wednesday may be regarded as no great loss to football. The sourness, even pain, in the circumstances is that there is a distinct feeling of relief that the Argentinians have gone. Football loses all meaning when we reach the stage of being glad to call it off.

The recent history of the game as contested between Argentina and Britain is indeed distressingly ugly. Between the sending off of Rattin at Wembley in the 1966 World Cup and the simultaneous dismissals of George Best and Medina at Old Trafford on Wednesday night we have suffered Celtic's three gruesomely vengeful matches against Racing last year and then that spiteful first leg of this year's tie between Estudiantes and Manchester United in Buenos Aires. The game has never looked more nasty or more trivial.

Yet Sir Matt Busby, United's manager, is being honest to his professional nature when he shakes his grey head and smiles sadly, as he did at his press conference after Wednesday's return match, and insists that "you can't run away from these things.'

Busby's view is the true competitor's: if the challenge exists it must be met. The fact that this particular event is really only a spectacle and not a logical competition is irrelevant to the committed contestant. It is at the moment the only World Club Championship we have.

Wednesday's match, a 1-1 draw to give Estudiantes the title on an aggregate of 2-1, was neither the brawl that some feared nor the uncomprehending collision of opposites that others promised. An English team lacking in organisation and individually short of form was cleverly, resolutely contained by a South American one thoroughly prepared for a specific exercise in defence and counter attack.

The difference was in method, not in moral basis. Certainly the Argentinians tackled with a ferocious abandon, the weight of the body following through behind the kick aimed only roughly at the ball. Certainly they were well tutored in the techniques of irritation; arguing at every opportunity; intent on holding up the flow of the game. But none of that was being seen by the Old Trafford crowd for the first time, the Football League has several clubs with a talent for all of it.

The game was more of a bore than a disgrace. United, a goal behind within six minutes, never found enough pace, accuracy or invention to master this cynical, composed opposition.

The match rushed headlong into its double climax: Best's and Medina's sending off for fighting, with Medina being pushed and punched into submission by his own trainer, and then United's goal.

Later a group of Estudiantes players and officials arrived in the press room for no other reason, it seemed, than to give a brief, relished chanting of their club's and their country's names in the presence of men they believed had wickedly abused them. They grinned at us in proud rebuke.

By then both Busby and his team had conceded without hedging that the better side had won the title. But that admission did not end the bitterness created by the first match. Best, his lower lip purple and ridged, said the following day: "It's no good saying, 'Well, perhaps they weren't such a dirty side after all.' They *are* dirty. There's such a lot goes on that doesn't get noticed. Dave Sadler's gone off to the dentist this morning with two teeth hanging half out and his mouth all swollen up. He was punched. Who knew about that?"

Best was looking at the evening newspaper report of his banning from United's next two European Cup matches against Anderlecht in punishment for his fight with Medina. He said he thought to be banned for one match would have been severe enough. Medina, he said, had elbowed him in the mouth as he walked past. "I just hit him back."

Medina, of course, in the well-drilled way of the Argentinians, went down as if he had been struck by a bus, just as Estudiantes' captain and Best's marker, Malbernat, had done earlier when slapped by the Irishman.

This particular incident went unremarked by the referee, and Best would not talk about it. But I saw Malbernat stride five or six paces towards Best and spit in his face. Best's reply was delayed for two or three seconds. Malbernat stood facing him, as if waiting to be struck. When he was he fell elaborately.

It was plain enough that the Argentinians had the measure of Best's brittle irritability. Ironically, it was a night when they had no need to rile him. He played poorly, and afterwards said so without prevarication. "I never got going at all. It's been like that for two or three matches now. It was just bad that it had to happen for this big game."

Best's frank displeasure at himself can perhaps serve as the comment on this World Club Championship. The event needs time to change. It would be no kind of treatment to suppress it.

Guardian, 20 October 1968

MISTER BEST COMES TO TOWN
Jenny Pearson

George Best is as elusive off the football field as on it. With three alternative telephone numbers, you might imagine it easy enough to find him. Not at all. Like Macavity the Mystery Cat, he has an uncanny way of evaporating seconds before you ring.

It took three days and nine telephone calls to catch up with him – at his boutique in the Village area of Manchester: the little King's Road of the north. A guarded, formal voice said: "MISTER Best here." When he realised I was not a pursuant fan the voice became less cagey, more Irish. He agreed to meet me on United's next visit to London. The coach would arrive at 4 p.m.; would I give him an hour or so to freshen up and then meet him at the team's Bloomsbury hotel?

The day came and, wearing a red dress in honour of Manchester United, I was in the old-fashioned hallway at 5 p.m., half expecting him to enter in the grand manner down the imposing stairway. Such was his overblown image in my mind's eye: the young god of the soccer world on the one hand and the teenagers on the other, whose obvious star quality and sharp, know-it-all comments in the press made him an alarming subject to interview. So there I stood, awaiting the descent from Olympus.

Some other United players walked by, chatting about a film they were going to see as Denis Law steered them towards a waiting taxi. Then George Best appeared at a side door, smiling with an odd mixture of shyness and conspiratorial friendliness as he crossed the room towards me. He is marvellous to look at, but not as one expects a footballer: a matador, perhaps, or a dancer. The deep-set, blue eyes sparkle with an amused look, as though seeing the joke beneath the surface of things. At the same time, he was uneasy. He glanced after the others and I was suddenly reminded of a boy left behind by a school outing for an unpleasant interview with the headmaster.

We drank tea – "my favourite drink, if you want to know" – and he tucked into a large plate of sandwiches. Two large plates, to be accurate. He was monosyllabic, hiding behind small neat hands – a small red jewel flashing from one, a diamond from the other.

We talked of the big match next day. Was he apprehensive? No. George never suffers from the stage fright that assails so many, even the greatest. Half an hour before kick-off, when others are already changed and a 60,000 crowd is building up on the terrace of Old Trafford, he is invariably to be found drinking tea in a public bar near the dressing rooms, cool and unconcerned. His unflappability, deeply valued by Sir Matt, is a joke among friends who hustle him off to change when he has apparently forgotten all about the coming match.

I asked if anything ever made him nervous. Shrinking into the soft folds of his jacket he replied: "Yes. This. Being interviewed by a girl." That sounded pretty funny from someone reputed to move around in a cloud of girls. Anyway, it broke the ice.

He was soon talking quite freely about his life in the limelight, about its effect on his private life, about his abiding love for football. In conversation, the soft Irish voice rounds the edges off statements that cut more harshly in black and white: "I don't believe in tactics . . . I play as I feel . . . No one ever taught me how to play." His eyes light up as he defends the cause of the free imaginative approach to football: the brand of game played by United. No wonder it is a popular parlour game to picture this most unpredictable of performers in the England team of Sir Alf Ramsey, the meticulous strategist whose methods he has attacked in print. But then, as Sir Alf witheringly observed when the subject was raised in conversation, "It's impossible. He's Irish."

A controversial figure, George at 22 stands poised as it were between heaven and hell. Chosen, on the one hand, as the youngest ever Footballer of the Year and the only Briton chosen for the Rest of the World side to play Brazil next week (although injury will now prevent his playing), he is simultaneously under heavy fire for misbehaviour on the field.

Yet there is really nothing tricky or enigmatic about Best himself. The touchstone of his being is and always has been a passionate love of football. He even gave up a place in a rugby-playing grammar school to attend a secondary modern where soccer was the code.

Perhaps it is in this very love for the game that his temperamental weakness lies: the free-flying joy of it that takes him weaving and dancing through the web of defence.

He plays with the dedication of an artist. Even now, he says: "I hate Sundays because there is no football. I would like to cut Sundays out of the week altogether." I asked, half expecting a shrug or a laugh, if he saw football as an art form. He thought seriously for a few seconds and replied, "Yes. If I see anyone playing it wrong, in an international match or a kids' game in the park, I get angry."

I asked if he was still homesick for Ireland and his family, for homesickness nearly caused him to abandon his career with Manchester United in the early days. "Yes," he said. It was a mournful, faraway reply. "Our youngest is only two and when I go home he doesn't recognise me." He can hardly ever get to Ireland during the season. His younger brother and sisters are by now more familiar with his public image than with George himself.

Mrs Best told me, "Sometimes we say to our youngest, 'Where's George?' and he goes to imitate him, holding a ball above his head with both hands. But he doesn't realise it's his brother!"

George talks brightly about famous people he has got to know: "It's amazing, when you're a footballer the people who love you. Albert Finney, now. He's a great actor, nearly a millionaire, and he's bloody football daft!" But with ordinary people there are barriers, everywhere there are people trying to use him, from people with business propositions down to the minor nuisance of autograph hunters: he has an extraordinary knack of signing his name one-handed and half behind his back without a pause in his conversation. It all goes some way to explain that wary, almost hunted look.

Success has brought a lot of fun and wealth, but it has also cut him off from much that is dear and familiar. He says that friends back home seem to think because he is famous that he must be big-headed. "I have two or three friends I love going to see, but I get the uncomfortable feeling they think I'm going out of politeness. They think I'm changed, but I'm not. If they're going to a local dance they don't even ask me. I'd love to go, but they think it's too low for me."

If you measure his newspaper image it is under-standable. The views proclaimed in his name are not exactly modest. What you miss in reading them is the whole aura of the person: the brooding, withdrawn quality, and the sudden flashes of quick wit, watching to see if it is well taken. Opinions thus drawn out of him by journalists and ghost writers are strung together under his name, making fluent, opinionated pronounce-ments that are quite out of character.

It is his feet that speak the magic: but the world requires him also to be an oracle. Perhaps the world gets what it deserves. George Best, left to speak for himself, merely spins up a coin in his favourite pub, kicks it over his shoulder from the underside of his foot and lands it neatly in a friend's breast pocket. Then he does it again to show it wasn't a fluke. That's his view of life in a nutshell. Then he turns to you, black eyebrows shooting up in laughter, and says: "Have a drink, luv. What would you like?"

Observer, 3 November 1968

GEORGE BACK AT HIS BEST
Arthur Hopcraft

Manchester United: 2
Wolverhampton Wanderers: 0

Diffident and ragged for the first half hour, when they could not deal with the disruptive wit of this Wolves side, Manchester managed a laboured recovery both of confidence and of a measure of their highly distinctive aptitudes.

Best's goal, which he had been promising with startling hints and coy near-misses, had all the thrill that goes with his most insistent talent; Law's was scored with one of those leaping headers which made his intimidating reputation.

But if Manchester ended with a degree of arrogance, there had been plenty in the game to alarm their fans into an intermittent grumbling.

Dougan's mastery of Sadler, looking half-paced and hesitant, threatened early on to cripple the Manchester defence decisively. Bailey, Woodfield and Parkin were allowed so much ease in containing a dull-edged Manchester attack that they had time to prompt their own forwards with care.

Wolves, in the first half, might well have profited abundantly from a far more optimistic attitude. With great physical strength and a general diligence this side may well be the best the Wolverhampton club has had for three or four seasons. But it looks over concerned with its organisation.

Could it have achieved a more ready adaptability here, Wolves might have exploited Manchester's seriously vague covering in defence, instead of merely exposing it embarrassingly.

After 20 minutes Dougan, bursting away from Sadler, brought a fine save from Stepney of the vital kind that had yet to be demanded from Parkes. And 10 minutes later Sadler had to hook Dougan down deliberately from behind as the centre forward reached the edge of the Manchester penalty area.

The weak point of Manchester's defence had been made glaringly obvious. But from then on it was, barely believable, to be left hardly tested.

Wolves lost Woodfield 10 minutes before the interval, after he had been injured when trying to cut short Best's run to the right of the Wolverhampton goal.

Woodfield's absence had a markedly diminishing effect on Wolves' solidity, and in the last five minutes before the interval Manchester at last found the space and time they needed to mount clear-cut attacks.

The first half ended with a header from Best which was narrowly wide and another from Law which was only just palmed away under the bar by Parkes. From the moment the second half opened, with Wignall taking Woodfield's place and Kenning coming on as an extra midfield player, Manchester's greater fluency and directness began to claim them a distinct authority.

Exactly on the hour, Manchester's new certainty made its first killing impact. Crerand cut through the Wolves defence with a 30 yard ground pass which found Best closely attended by Parkin, but not too closely to restrain the gifts which allow him to capitalise on half chances of this kind. Parkin matched Best's speed in the run towards goal, but as Best halted a feint to the right destroyed Parkin's balance and Best, moving abruptly to his left, hit the ball hard past Parkes as the goalkeeper hurried from his goal.

From now until the end, Best's personality was to dominate the play. He was avid for the ball as he has not been all this season, and he was inventive in its use far beyond his form for many matches. He worked through very nearly the whole range of his talents: complicated dribbling, sudden long passes, unexpected leaps and headers.

The change in the Wolves side reflected all this. The

whole calibre of the Manchester play now seemed a little beyond Wolves' class.

Ten minutes from the end Law scored a goal worthy of his past. Charlton sent Morgan scurrying away on the left, Morgan delayed his cross until he reached the byline, and Law rose near the far post to head fiercely into the net.

Manchester United: Stepney; Kopel, Dunne, Crerand, Sadler, Stiles, Morgan, Sartori, Charlton, Law, Best. **Sub**: Fitzpatrick.
Wolverhampton Wanderers: Parkes; Parkin, Thompson, Bailey, Woodfield, Holsgrove, Wignall, Knowles, Dougan, Wilson, Wagstaffe. **Sub**: Kenning.

Observer, 1 December 1968

SHANKLY'S MEN FIND THEIR FEET TOO LATE
Hugh McIlvanney

Manchester United: 1
Liverpool: 0

On a frozen field, where even the most graceful players began by scurrying around with their arms spread and their feet close together, like penguins, United's skills were severely compromised and Liverpool's athletic momentum almost a liability.

Signs that frustration would be the currency of the bleak afternoon came early with the sight of Best and Charlton slithering like novice skaters as they steadied to collect simple passes. Thompson, who normally seems able to go from a gallop into full reverse, was equally discomforted. One could almost see the asterisks in the balloons of breath that formed above the players' heads.

Yet the match emerged as marvellously exciting and

not merely because hectic commitment compensated for the absence of composed aggression. Talent kept breaking through and if most of it belonged to United, Liverpool sustained their challenge with enough spirit to produce a daunting crescendo in the last 10 minutes.

There had been some frantic changing of boots at the interval, but that late surge probably owed more to physical strength than footwear. At last, as the opposition tired, Mr Shankly's big men started to lose their resemblance to the Grand Fleet at Jutland and find a destructive sprightliness.

But there was too little time in which to erase the supremacy United had built up in the middle hour of the game. In that period, only St John, superbly unimpressed by the conditions, gave Liverpool hope of cohesion. Yeats was splendidly assured and Callaghan hustled with admirable determination, but the rest laboured painfully against a United who wrestled with their wintry problem until they achieved their best form of the season.

Best struggled doggedly until he was able to impose at least a measure of his class, Charlton and Crerand refused to accept that this was an afternoon when their touch should be invalidated by treacherous bounces. Stiles and the gifted newcomer Sartori, whose short choppy actions were a natural advantage, adjusted even sooner.

With James, the immensely promising 18-year-old centre half, they made vital contributions to a victory that must have been clearer had Lawrence not chosen to give another of his heroically defiant performances. Lawrence, who could not go down to feet more often if he had a shoeshine concession, obviously had a lot to do with the record of eight games without defeat – four without the loss of a goal – that Liverpool carried into this match.

On such a day one slip or one fortuitous deflection might be conclusive. Almost immediately it seemed that Manchester were to have the decisive break. Smith, bulkily vulnerable, lost his footing as he prepared to pass to Lawrence and when Sadler converged with the goalkeeper, the ball bounced agonisingly only inches wide.

The next chance was more deliberately contrived by Sadler. Exhibiting a sudden contempt for the pitch, he skipped elegantly past Smith, and Sartori responded to this pass by turning the ball back swiftly from the corner flag. But the frost had the last word when Law made a skidding swing and missed his shot completely.

The fight for composure was clearly going United's way and Best's 20 yard shot on the run, or rather on the stumble, forced Lawrence to make a good save. Liverpool's most promising retaliation came, unsurprisingly, from St John. He lunged in to beat Crerand for a ball just outside United's area, but the instant half-volley was caught confidently by Stepney as he dived to his left.

However, most of the action, on and off the field, was near Lawrence. He was defending the goal at the Stretford end and before long the police were dragging handfuls of pugilistic spectators from the terraces behind him.

The more legitimate violence was still being threatened by United. With the interval about five minutes away, Best swung outside Lawler with all the familiar casual ease, but he could not control his feet as Yeats challenged and the chance was lost. There were others to come. An intelligent wide pass from right to left by Sartori left Smith like a man treading water, and Best sprinted for goal. But the collision with the hurtling mass of Lawrence came too soon. The goalkeeper had to make a similarly courageous interception on Sadler and again to thwart Best and Sartori before half time brought him respite.

United did not have to wait long in the second half to take reward for their pressure. They had one disappointment when a powerful volley by Crerand was competently saved but in the 53rd minute they scored a splendid goal. Charlton was by now an encouragingly creative influence and it was his curving 30 yard pass that set Best free of imminent challenge on the right. As Yeats closed to tackle it seemed that Best would take him on, but Law had just appealed for smarter service and Best complied brilliantly. His left-footed cross was a cunning inswinger and it curled to bounce behind Lawler and in front of Law. There was only one feasible culmination then and Law's thrusting header provided it.

Liverpool, inevitably, made a final rally and Thompson twice almost earned the equaliser. He finished one great run with a shot that went narrowly wide and then gave St John an inviting pass in the inside-left position. Stepney fumbled the shot at first and recovered in time to prevent a hundred heart attacks.

Manchester United: Stepney; Dunne, Burns, Crerand, James, Stiles, Best, Sadler, Charlton, Law, Sartori.
Liverpool: Lawrence; Lawler, Strong, Smith, Yeats, Hughes, Callaghan, Hunt, Evans, St John, Thompson.

Observer, 15 December 1968

BEST AN EXCEPTION TO RULE
Paul Wilcox

Leeds United: 2
Manchester United: 2

If Manchester United did not have George Best, they would not have much. They should be thankful that Best takes no heed of the dictum that football is a team game where smooth, collective effort pays richer dividends than the spurts of individual brilliance. Two spurts on Saturday: two goals; one valuable point.

Best is the exception to the rule, of course, but without him, who would score the crucial goals? Charlton is playing deeper than ever, Morgan has lost his early-season flair, Givens and Gowling at the moment have not the experience, and Kidd has not emulated the scoring feats he achieved with the reserves. There is Law, but Law and a question mark have been companions for some time now. Manchester United need a goal poacher – but poachers are hard to catch even at today's huge rewards.

Leeds United also have problems. Their team work and ability to score cannot usually be faulted at Elland Road; but they lacked the lustre, the killer instinct which typified their Championship run last season. Don Revie as usual said: "I refuse to criticise my players in public." But the inference was that in private there would be a few strong words – Jones, Madeley, Bremner, and Hunter probably excepted – for a side which has dropped six points in five matches.

Good intelligent football was evident: but it was football in slow motion. "Posed by models for spot-the-ball photographers" would have been a worthy caption for the early scenes, so many were the times that the ball was booted high into the air with players looking in all directions. And in one of these scenes Leeds took the lead when Giles put a long pass up the middle. Sadler climbed high and headed into his own net.

The second half was brighter, almost enjoyable, because of the opportunism of Best and Bremner. Best equalised from close range after running into the right position at the right time, and then put Manchester ahead in a rare and decisive move. He shot from 20 yards through three defenders and the ball entered the net off the inside of a post. Bremner levelled the scores with a magnificent overhead kick

which deceived Stepney, who had enjoyed a return to
his best form.

Leeds United: Sprake; Reaney, Cooper, Bremner, J Charlton, Hunter,
Madeley, Lorimer, Jones, Giles, Gray. **Sub**: O'Grady.
Manchester United: Stepney; Fitzpatrick, Dunne, Burns, Ure, Sadler,
Morgan, Givens, R. Charlton, Gowling, Best.
Referee: J. Finney (Hereford).

Guardian, 8 September 1969

WEST HAM ARE LEFT CHASING BEST'S SHADOW
Paul Wilcox

Manchester United: 5
West Ham United: 2

Manchester United can begin thinking about winning
the League Championship again. Twelve points from
their last eight games still leaves them eight points
behind the leaders; but what does that matter when
confidence has returned, each member of the team
wants the ball, and is discharging his allotted duty in
football as varied as it is brilliant, and collectively they
can beat a fine West Ham United side 5-2.

The margin may have been slightly flattering, but
victory was richly deserved. Apart from a brief nig-
gling phase, the match was memorable for both teams
placing the accent on football, with West Ham's plan of
attack allowing Manchester to play their own inventive game. But the difficulty of trying to arrange plans
in advance – whether to attack or to defend – is like
that of trying to organise a foolproof system of traffic
control. The human element lets you down.

The human element which destroyed West Ham's
hopes of unsettling Manchester by their powerful

assaults was in the shape of George Best, whose occasional skills and grace left opponents tackling his ever-disappearing shadow. By Best's incredible standards, he did not have a great game. However, he headed two goals by out-leaping taller defenders, and fashioned another out of nothing for Kidd.

Victory was earned by matter-of-fact utilitarian principles rather than the conscious striving for the artistry of Best. Where much of Manchester's strength lay was with their half-backs – Ure, the morale booster; Burns, who has found his true position in taking over Crerand's duties so effectively; and Sadler, who is playing with a consistency bordering on brilliance. From these three flowed best-bib-and-tucker football, although Sadler was lectured for a foul and Lampard received his second booking in three weeks. Lampard's way of stopping Morgan was modelled too closely on Samson's in the temple for the referee's taste.

It was unfortunate that West Ham lost by so many goals after playing so well. Backed by the superb Moore, Lindsay worked hard without any reward for his entertaining industry. He had Stepney beaten with a fierce drive, but the ball hit the crossbar. Another Best, called Clyde, a bonny-looking centre forward from Bermuda, took enough weight off Hurst to enable the latter twice to reduce Manchester's lead to one goal. After 26 minutes Hurst headed home a lob by Redknapp, and with the score at 3-1, headed past Stepney, following a precision centre from Clyde Best.

Burns opened the scoring in the fifth minute, heading into the net from a corner by Aston. Seven minutes later, George Best headed the glorious second from Morgan's centre. Manchester's third was by Charlton, who had not scored since the opening day of the season, and Best scored the fourth after Aston's quick thinking and willingness to chase what looked to be a dead ball. Best, engineering a passing space between three defenders by his ability to turn in confined space, made the fifth for Kidd, who bounded forward to shoot past Ferguson.

Manchester United: Stepney; Fitzpatrick, Dunne, Burns, Ure, Sadler, Morgan, Kidd, Charlton, Aston, Best (G.).
West Ham United: Ferguson; Bonds, Lampard, Howe, Stephenson, Moore, Redknapp, Lindsay, Best (C.), Hurst, Peters.
Referee: R. Tinkler (Boston).

Guardian, 29 September 1969

BEST'S PRIVATE THOUGHTS
Hugh McIlvanney

"If I had been born ugly you'd never have heard of Pelé."

George Best smiled at his eloquent *non sequitur*. "But seriously, I know I would be a far better player than I am if I became as obsessed with the game as some fellows are. It just so happens that the way I'm made – and let's face it, the way I look has a lot to do with this – takes me into many other things in life. I get on very well with birds and I'm not one to fight against that.

"I like to enjoy myself, to get pleasure out of the money I'm making. It just wouldn't be possible for me to live like a monk to suit the demands of football. I love the game and I work hard at it, but I don't kid myself that I give it absolutely everything I could.

"When you ask me if I consider myself the best player in the world the answer is no. But I'm sure I could be. When I'm right at my sharpest I feel I can do anything with the ball whatever the opposition. What I'm saying is not smugness. How could I ever show the least contempt for football after what it's done for me? All I'm saying is that I could never narrow my life down to the point where the only thing that mattered was the game."

Players of the centre-parting era, who were often treated like the inmates of a reform school and paid a weekly wage that would not see Best through the first hour of a night out, should not be too eager to sneer at the attitudes he expressed when I spent a day with him in London last week. He is, without question, exposed to more formidable distractions than any other British footballer in history.

Everyone accepts that he has transcended the normal limitations of a sports reputation, emerging not only as a folk hero but almost as a cult in himself. To an incredible percentage of the population the name "Georgie" is unambiguous identification.

When he visits a nightclub or a discothèque in London, film stars and others reckoned to be First Division celebrities crowd round him. He seems sure to appear in feature films fairly soon, admitting that he was seriously tempted by the offer of a part in *The Virgin Soldiers*.

"I nearly did it, but it meant something like six months in Singapore. Even at that I thought about it but I realised it would be such a terrible disruption of my football career that it was never really on. But so much is happening these days that it's easy to get confused about your priorities."

Obviously, at 23, Best must be careful to avoid being buried under the golden apples before he can pluck them. He insists that he is in no immediate danger of being buried under a mountain of money.

Guesses about his gross income would clearly have to start on the other side of £20,000 a year; he is having a house built outside Manchester that will eventually present him with a bill for £30,000; he drives a very fancy Lotus. Yet, despite all this and the tycoon image fostered by press stories about his business interests, he says rather ruefully that he has very little money to hand. "People think I've got fortunes. Well, I'm not pleading poverty. I'm living well. But I've got no real money in the bank, nothing that would impress anybody."

He is equally at pains to correct the assumption that he has troops of friends. "If there are three or four people I can regard as real friends that's the lot." He has his mother's deep-set eyes (indeed nearly all his physical features are inherited from her side of the family) and often in a crowd they take on a look of extreme remoteness. People and their antics wash around him without seriously impinging on his private thoughts.

"I don't find it easy to get really close to people or maybe I should say I don't find it easy to let them get really close to me. I've got a great relationship with my family, of course, but I've been away from home since I was 15.

"A lot of the other people I come in contact with I've learned to suspect because I know how little their friendship means. But I'm not suggesting that's the full explanation of why I can count my friends on one hand.

"The thing is that I don't really need other people all that much, at least I don't have to lean on them emotionally. In fact, when I feel I'm getting involved it makes me uneasy."

His recent highly publicised experience with a Danish girl friend may be taken as illustration of this, but he quotes an earlier episode as a vivid example. It concerned a girl in London whom he had admired for some time from afar, which is scarcely his regular form. Ultimately they came into enthusiastic collision, spent a couple of marvellously hectic days together and arranged to meet again the following morning.

"She was coming round to pick me up at the place where I was staying but suddenly I got out of bed, packed and took off for Manchester. I left a note on the door for her. It said: 'Nobody knows me.'"

George Best is honest enough to include himself in that statement.

Observer, 30 November 1969

BEST SUFFERS A SEVERE PENALTY FOR FOOLISHNESS
Eric Todd

George Best, successful business man and footballer extraordinary, has been suspended for a month and fined £100 by the FA Disciplinary Committee. United in general and Best in particular thus were in a state of confessed shock when they left Manchester for today's FA Cup tie at Ipswich. It will be interesting to see whether Best can fulfil his promise to turn in one of his more bewildering performances before he goes into enforced retirement.

The alleged offence for which Best has been punished occurred at the end of the first leg match of the Football League Cup semi-final against Manchester City at Maine Road. As the players left the field Best – who earlier in the evening had been cautioned by the referee, Mr J. K. Taylor, of Wolverhampton, for time wasting – knocked the ball out of the referee's hands. He was arraigned for conduct likely to bring the game into disrepute or, as it used to be known, "ungentlemanly conduct." Best did not ask for a personal hearing at the Disciplinary Committee meeting.

Like many Irishmen, Best is quick on the draw, so to say, when in trouble – as a genius he suffers more than most from tough treatment by opponents – but on the whole he suffers indignity tolerably well. He has had five bookings spread over seven seasons with United; he was sent off in the World Club Championship match against Estudiantes at Old Trafford where patience all round was stretched to its limits. For the rest Best, like Caesar's wife, Bobby Charlton, and one or two more, has been above suspicion. His caution at Maine Road was his first this season.

It is a good thing that the Disciplinary Committee should not differentiate between the exalted and the humble when making their decisions. An offence is an offence be it committed by master or serf, in the First Division or in some minor league. It is no less gratifying that the Committee seemingly considers that any gesture which undermines or flaunts authority is as heinous as a foul or any other unfair tactic.

No rational person would deny that the referee was right to report Best for his foolish action. But how many, like me, wonder whether Mr Taylor might have been inclined to overlook the incident or even to play it down if the game had not been televised. Pat Crerand was another player whose spitting at an opponent on the field of play was seen by thousands on television.

Television is an inconsistent witness at football matches, recording as often as not only what it thinks the public should see. Sometimes it is not even there. My own view is that if television is to be subpoenaed or used indirectly, either as a witness for the defence or for the prosecution, then it should present the case in full, not merely in extracts. Otherwise the referee, as the man in sole charge, should be left alone to administer the law as he thinks fit or, more important, as he is instructed so to do.

In the meantime, the overall financial loss involved will embarrass Best no more than it would Barbara Hutton or Lord Thomson of Fleet. On the other hand he will miss at least three League matches and possibly a Cup replay. Before he transgresses and gets himself suspended, a player of Best's quality and powers of attraction should ponder on the effect that his absence will have on his colleagues and on the attendances at those grounds where people pay to see him. And thereby help to pay his wages.

Guardian, 3 January 1970

BEST IS THE MASTER IN THE MUD
Albert Barham

Northampton Town: 2
Manchester United: 8

The day will long be remembered in Northampton, as George Best stripped the fantasy from this fifth round of the FA Cup competition to demonstrate that skill, individual and collective, has no substitute anywhere.

It is also a costly day for the local folk, 21,771 having had to pay the high price of £17,438 for the privilege of watching a massacre in the mud. While that massacre was led by one of the world's great forwards, it was contributed to by a sorry performance by Northampton, for whom nothing would go right.

Six goals out of eight is a remarkable revelation of skill on a surface which easily reflected the watery sun, and quickly churned into a morass. It put Best among the select who have scored six goals in a cup tie – Rooke, of Fulham, Atkinson, of Tranmere Rovers, and Hilsden, of Chelsea – but one short of the record of seven scored back in 1922 by Bill Minter in the fourth qualifying round. He gained all seven of St Albans' goals, and they were beaten 8-7 by Dulwich Hamlet. Which reminds me that Denis Law once scored six goals in a cup tie; not one of which counted. That was in the 1961 season, when a match against Luton was abandoned with Manchester City leading 6-2.

Best's scoring feat is remarkable in that it was achieved on the day he returned after a month's suspension, and filled with dread that United, who had been winning without him, would lose this one. "I hope the score is not a flash in the pan, but I really wanted to do something like this on my return," he said. Best certainly looked as though he needed the practice which Northampton so generously provided for him.

It is still a feat of great individual prowess, but it could not have been achieved without great team support, particularly from Brian Kidd, who scored the other goals, the mature wisdom of Crerand, and the busy workmanship of Sartori and Morgan.

Yet the County Ground, on Saturday, held the feeling that here was a ground where an upset might be possible. That impression lasted for 20 minutes. By then, Northampton, rumbling forward through the mud with their heavy brigade in full support, had missed a couple of chances. One had come from the busy Fairbrother, the other from Felton, with a long, speculative lob. But the old heads and the wise heads of Crerand and Charlton, and the increasingly accurate heading of Sadler and, particularly, Ure, calmed, soothed and settled United. Here was one of the great turning points of the game, and Northampton had lost it.

There is a wealth of understanding between Kidd and Best, and the manner in which Crerand first punished McNeil, then Rankmore for their mistakes allowed this understanding to blossom, and brought the first two goals, Best outjumping the defence, oddly enough, to head the first. The rest were more orthodox, and the fourth probably the hardest. By that time the Northampton defence had lost a lot of confidence, but there was still spirit. Edwards, with a rugged tackle on McNeil, conceded a penalty. Stepney pushed Rankmore's kick against the post, and saved again as Fairbrother thundered in to hit the rebounding ball at him. That was the second turning point, and again Northampton had lost out.

The rest, from then on, was mere formality, Best and Kidd completing the tally of eight goals, Best beginning at the rate of one goal every 10 minutes, then halving it as the game wore on. And Charlton, it was decided, should come off after 25 minutes of the second half. With his first kick of the ball, Burns, the substitute, provided Best with a pass to score his fifth goal. At the end, Northampton scored twice, the first by McNeil, then a header by Large.

Best likes adulation, but not the mobbing. For the last 30 seconds of this game he lurked within a couple of yards of the entrance to the dressing-room, and was first to the sanctuary as the final whistle brought crowds shrieking to reach the players.

Northampton Town: Book; Fairfax, Brookes, Clarke, Rankmore, Kiernan, Felton, Ross, Large, Fairbrother, McNeil.
Manchester United: Stepney; Edwards, Dunne, Crerand, Ure, Sadler, Morgan, Sartori, Charlton, Kidd, Best. **Sub**: Burns.
Referee: P. Baldwin (Middlesbrough).

Guardian, 9 February 1970

TIME NOW FOR A REST FOR BEST
Eric Todd

Manchester United: 0
Leeds United: 1

The long drawn out modernised tale of the two cities of Leeds and Manchester ended on Thursday night at Burnden Park. And, like Sidney Carton before him, Billy Bremner did a far, far better thing than he had ever done before – except perhaps at Nottingham in the FA Challenge Cup replayed semi-final in 1965, when his goal terminated Manchester United's ambitions.

This year, his acclamation as the hero was deferred until the third chapter.

So Leeds United, aspiring to a triple crown, will meet Chelsea in the final a fortnight hence. Those observers who still shudder when they remember Leeds United's two previous appearances at Wembley may feel disposed to pass a vote of censure on the men from Old Trafford, but they could be agreeably surprised. Leeds are a different side these days although their endurance will be taxed severely by a quite terrifying programme.

In many ways, Thursday's confrontation was the least satisfying of the three. The weather was fine and dry, but a strong wind subverted judgment and many a pass went astray. In the second half Leeds just booted the ball, chased it, and hoped.

The major difference was that for the first time in the three games, Leeds took the initiative and their early goal was something for which Manchester had not bargained. Manchester thereafter were unable to wrest the control as Leeds had done at Hillsborough and Villa Park and, while Yorkshiremen prayed for a second goal "to make sure," Lancastrians wondered anxiously who had the inventiveness to score for Manchester.

The build-up on both sides was slow and individual brilliance could not compensate for the absence of collective purpose. Leeds had no consistent forward and they were indebted chiefly to their defenders, among whom Jack Charlton, Cooper, and Bremner were outstanding. The feeling persisted that Leeds, with so much on their plates, had decided to give no more than they needed to. And who could blame them?

Bobby Charlton as an all-rounder had no equal and even Leeds supporters felt sorry for him as his stupendous output in attack and defence went to waste. He coaxed, drove and raged (which was unusual for him) but, like Leeds, Manchester were only fitful in their approach and again like Leeds, Manchester were given best service by their defenders notably Sadler, Edwards, and the quite irrepressible Stiles.

Best again made no impact. He is going through lean days and nobody blames him for that. It happens to us all, rich and poor. Nevertheless, his considerable name and reputation should not be guarantees of automatic selection, and to the patriots' insistence that "they can't drop Georgie" the reply surely must be, "Why not?" A period of contemplation in some retreat could do him a lot of good there to sort out the various problems which seemingly beset him. He'll be back.

The goal arrived after eight minutes. Lorimer centred, Clarke – who did little else – headed the ball down, it struck Jones on the shin and broke to Bremner who drove it magnificently with his left foot past Stepney.

Leeds United: Sprake; Reaney, Cooper, Bremner, J. Charlton, Madeley, Lorimer, Clarke, Jones, Giles, Gray.
Manchester United: Stepney; Edwards, Dunne, Crerand, Sadler, Stiles, Morgan, Sartori, R. Charlton, Kidd, Best. **Sub**: Law.
Referee: J. K. Taylor (Wolverhampton).

Guardian, 28 March 1970

BEST GIVES UNITED THE EDGE
Eric Todd

Manchester United: 2
Chelsea: 1

If Manchester United are on the way out, as some people imagine – or hope – they are, then they intend taking their time about it. Against expectation, they beat Chelsea 2-1 in their Football League Cup fourth-round match last night at Old Trafford and gave notice that they are a long way from being finished as a power in the land.

In any case while there is Best there is hope and so long as he stays at Old Trafford, United can never be written off. The same is true of one or two others of course, but Best is unique, and not only as the owner-occupier of one of the most desirable residences in the country. Take last night for example.

Chelsea, playing some brilliant football, had equalised Charlton's goal and they were set fair to do even better. Then in the 70th minute Best, who was just inside the Chelsea half, called to Aston to give him the ball. Aston is not one to ignore such a request and he put through a perfect pass.

Off went Best with the redoubtable Harris in stern pursuit. Twice Harris tried to bring him down from behind and twice Best eluded the tackle. Best next rounded Bonetti, stopped briefly to have a word with Hinton, who had appeared smartly, and then tapped the ball into the net. Insolence gone mad!

At the end of the game Osgood trooped off the field with an arm around Best's shoulder asking him no doubt for a few hints on magic for the beginner.

Best's goal possibly helped conceal one or two United deficiencies, which still persist in spite of last night's commendable performance. As I suggested, United are not yet finished but strengthening here and there will help delay the end which the pessimists forecast. Kidd, Sadler, Charlton and the magnificent Fitzpatrick all did more than their share in support of Best, and Rimmer made some good saves. But with Law having retired with an injury at half time the forwards as a unit did not quite match the consistent threat of the Chelsea attack.

Chelsea were unlucky perhaps not to have forced a replay. With Hutchinson and Cooke in top form, the Chelsea forwards moved briskly and intelligently and would have worn down lesser men than Fitzpatrick. They had a goal disallowed – rightly so as Hutchinson pushed James in his enthusiasm to score – and towards the end they gave all they had, but luck was against them.

When United were on the rampage, Hollins and Webb, both admirable marksmen as well as defenders, made no concessions and Bonetti like Rimmer gave a first-class exhibition in the art of goalkeeping. But is there a defence anywhere which has an antidote against Best in this mood?

Charlton gave United the lead after 30 minutes. Receiving the ball from Best on the left, he cut inside and, shooting from 25 yards, he beat Bonetti who appeared to be confounded by the way the ball skidded along the ground. Four minutes later Fitzpatrick headed the ball out and Hollins, racing in at a fair rate of knots, hit it first time along the ground and Rimmer had no hope of saving a goal.

Manchester United: Rimmer; Edwards, Dunne, Fitzpatrick, James, Sadler, Law, Best, Charlton, Kidd, Aston.
Chelsea: Bonetti; Mulligan, Harris, Hollins, Hinton, Webb, Weller, Cooke, Osgood, Hutchinson, Houseman.

Guardian, 29 October 1970

MAGICAL TOUCHES FROM BEST
Paul Wilcox

Manchester United: 3
West Bromwich Albion: 1

George Best last night performed a splendid one-man show to put Manchester United at the top of the First Division again. West Bromwich Albion suffered agonies as he went through his repertoire of tricks, seemingly determined to show what a farewell to United's enforced exile from Old Trafford should be like. Albion were destroyed and demoralised and it was all Best's doing.

He was magic personified, subjecting Albion to all sorts of miseries as well as scoring two of United's goals. The applause which he received at the end of each half was all that he deserved.

It is only sad for United that Best, in view of his disciplinary record, might not be able to help them for possibly three months. If he is suspended for that length of time, the game will lose something.

Albion were destroyed by Best's majesty. Only Astle and Brown presented any problem to a competent defence. But Stepney was always capable of halting their fleeting thrusts until the last minute, when Brown scored.

The rout began in the ninth minute. Best floated a precise centre to Kidd, but the ball hit Cumbes and went for a corner Albion were reprieved for only seconds. Charlton's corner kick was a half-hit effort, but Cantello missed the ball completely, Sadler flicked it on, and Best turned it into the net.

Best's control and timing were perfect, and United should have gone farther ahead when he cut Albion's defence to pieces once more with a devastating pass through the penalty area. Aston sadly fumbled the opportunity.

In the 37th minute Albion fell further behind when Best won a corner on the left, took the kick himself, centred to the massed penalty area, and Gowling soared to head the ball into the net. The third and best goal came after 57 minutes when Best rounded Wile to leave Cumbes with no chance with the shot which followed.

Trouble was minimal and only three arrests were made. The only thing that might have troubled United last night was the fact that they will have to pay about £1,200 in compensation because of a gate of only 23,146. The referee certainly had no trouble. Mr Hartley said afterwards: "The match was a pleasure to referee. All my decisions were accepted without question, and it appears that the tightening of the laws is having the desired effect."

Manchester United: Stepney; O'Neil, Dunn, Gowling, James, Sadler, Morgan, Kidd, Charlton, Best, Aston.
West Bromwich Albion: Cumbes; Hughes, Wilson, Cantello, Wile, Kaye, Suggett, Brown, Astle, Hope, Hartford.
Referee: G. Hartley (Wakefield).

Guardian, 25 August 1971

BEST IN MORE TROUBLE
Eric Todd

George Best of Manchester United has been suspended for two weeks by the club and fined a fortnight's wages – about £300. Best did not turn up for his confrontation with Sir Matt Busby at Old Trafford yesterday.

At the ground Sir Matt chose his words carefully when he made the announcement about Best's suspension – but he underlined one key phrase, that the penalty on Best is the maximum United could impose upon the player. The full text of the statement was: "George Best did not turn up for training this morning and has made no contact with the club. I have discussed the matter with my directors over the telephone and it has been decided to suspend the player for 14 days."

Best, dropped by Sir Matt from the team when he missed the train to London on Friday for the Chelsea game, was reported to have returned to Manchester by hire car yesterday. Then it was said that he was flying up this morning. But his business partner, Malcolm Mooney, who met the plane at Ringway Airport, was staggered to find Best not among the passengers.

Best has stressed recently that he does not want to leave the club who discovered him as a schoolboy. Sir Matt said at the weekend: "My door is always open to any member of my staff and if George has problems of any sort I will be delighted to discuss them with him and try to find a solution."

Best was fined £250 by the FA Disciplinary Committee last Monday, which means a loss of over £500 in a fortnight.

Few people will deny that Best got what was coming to him – some may feel that it was considerably less – regardless of the background to his irresponsible and disrespectful attitude towards his club. And few surely will suggest that he has been made a martyr.

This is no time for pious homilies but rather one for all managers, let alone Sir Matt Busby, to reflect on to what degree they are responsible when their players, and especially those in the top grade, go astray off the field as well as on it. Discipline must begin within the club no less than in the home, and if any employee shows wayward tendencies at 17 then the employer cannot reasonably complain if, having done nothing about it in the meantime, such tendencies persist at 23. The days when "Everyone should have more sense," appear to have vanished.

Best's professional, business, and social lives appear to be strangling one another, but Sir Matt, never one to despise a broken and contrite heart, no doubt will help him straighten things out.

In the meantime, Best has the talent if not the genius to fight his way back into the first team and into public esteem. If he has the temperament and the determination to do it, he will not lack for encouragement within

the club and beyond it. If he has neither, then
Manchester United and football in general will be all
the better for his absence.

Guardian, 12 January 1971

CHILDREN SWOOP ON HARASSED BEST
Malcolm Stuart

Manchester United's temporary loss was the Hanover
primary school's gain yesterday afternoon. Before the
final bell the word went round: "Georgie Best is down
the road." Within minutes about 100 children were
standing outside the flat of the actress Miss Sinead
Cusack in Noel Road, Islington, North London,
chanting: "We want Georgie."

Journalists had waited for hours in the cold, catching
an occasional glimpse of United's suspended player at a
first floor window of the small, modern block of flats
overlooking Regent's Canal. But the Hanover School
boys and girls were not prepared for a stake-out.

Suddenly the front door, controlled by an electric
lock, gave way. Cheering 10 and 11-year-olds surged
into the building and banged on Miss Cusack's door.
Two television crews followed them in.

As young heads started to poke out of the skylights
of the building a police car arrived, followed by a van
with its siren wailing. Eight policemen joined the crush
in the building and reluctant children were persuaded
to leave. Fifty-eight of them filed out through the door.

The police knocked at Miss Cusack's door. She came
out to say: "I want all these people away." A moment
later a reporter who had followed the police into the
building got the only interview of the day with Best. It
was brief and uninformative.

Minutes later, Best's business partner, Mr Malcolm

Mooney, and two other men arrived in a blue Jaguar. An hour later, Best finally emerged with Mr Mooney and one other man. Police held the crowd back as they ran to the car. Mr Mooney was last night reported to be driving Best back to Manchester. The friend who remained behind said: "George hopes to see Sir Matt tomorrow lunchtime."

Later, Miss Cusack said: "George is very upset and unhappy. I feel very tired and weary after what has happened during the last three days." Best arrived at Miss Cusack's flat on Saturday evening after arriving in London too late to play for United against Chelsea.

Miss Cusack, daughter of the Irish actor, Cyril Cusack, said: "His problems have nothing to do with romance. It's all football. We spent about seven hours talking on Saturday night."

Mr Mooney phoned Miss Cusack's flat yesterday morning to give the news that United had suspended the player without pay for two weeks.

In Manchester, United's manager, Sir Matt Busby, said in a statement: "George Best did not turn up for training this morning and we have had no contact with him. I have been in contact with my directors over the telephone and we have decided to suspend the player for 14 days as from today."

Mr Mooney said: "George is emotionally disturbed. I am very upset."

Guardian, 12 January 1971

BEST: "I WAS WRONG"
Albert Barham

George Best unburdened himself to Sir Matt Busby for half an hour yesterday and agreed to start afresh in the cause of the club.

Best, who had been suspended for two weeks – the maximum punishment – for failing to report for training and who had been dropped from the team to play at Chelsea on Saturday, will now go away for a few days before resuming training on Monday.

Before seeing Sir Matt at Old Trafford yesterday, Best said: "I am bitterly disappointed with the team's performances in the past month: it was the main reason I staged my protest. I certainly do not want to leave United – I want to see them at the top again." United won 2-1 at Stamford Bridge on Saturday, their first victory in 11 matches.

Sir Matt and Best smilingly emerged from their meeting. The manager said they had discussed Best's personal and private problems and now were the best of friends once more. "I am glad it is all over at last," said Best. "I have apologised to the boss for what I did, and now realise I went about things the wrong way. I went down to London to think things over and then the press trapped me inside the flat" (of Sinead Cusack his actress friend).

Guardian, 13 January 1971

LONG BAN LIKELY FOR BEST
Albert Barham

Chelsea: 2
Manchester United: 3

George Best was sent off the field after 43 minutes of Manchester United's match at Stamford Bridge last night after Willie Morgan had been cautioned. The incidents followed a goal by Baldwin when he headed in Osgood's pass.

Morgan protested to Norman Burtenshaw, the

referee, and was cautioned as a result of his remarks. As he was writing Morgan's name in his book Best came over and joined in the chat. As a result of what he said Mr Burtenshaw seemed to write his name in his book also, and as a consequence of further conversation sent Best from the field.

Mr Burtenshaw, who refereed the last Cup Final, has been involved in a number of controversies in his career. Most recently he reported the entire Benfica team to the FA for their behaviour during a match with Arsenal.

Best is already under a suspended sentence of six weeks following three cautions and now faces a long period out of the game when he appears before the Disciplinary Committee.

Up to that time the match had been rather a colourless affair dictated for the most part by the midfield players. Chelsea did most of the attacking early for, anxious as they were to redeem themselves after their disappointing display on Saturday, there was much more creative work from Hudson and Hollins. Though there were shots from Hollins and Baldwin it was after 20 minutes' play that the biggest cheer of the evening came. That was from a shot by Charlton. It was from well outside the penalty area and though Phillips got well behind it the crowd sensed and savoured the power and grace of the old master. Law also tried to break through as did Kidd and Best, but Harris and Dempsey seemed to have them well covered.

However, Chelsea were reprieved by the action of a linesman when Best wiggled through and his shot rebounded off Phillips' chest. Law was there to turn the ball into the net but was adjudged offside. Then came Chelsea's goal and the protestation which led to Best being sent off.

Chelsea in an attempt to press forward their advantage brought on Cooke in place of Houseman who had been injured in a collision with Kidd. But it was United and their spirit of recovery which captured the imagination of this crowd of almost 50,000, though they still had their own hero in Phillips. United were unlucky when Kidd saw Harris deflect away a shot which seemed a certain score. Then Morgan twice watched Phillips claw down his shots and Charlton himself was also foiled by the alacrity of this young goalkeeper.

But in the 67th minute Charlton swept the ball out to Dunne who beat a covey of Chelsea defenders before sending across the pass from which Kidd, with a sharp flick of the head, brought United level.

Three minutes later United scored again. Kidd was put through the defence. He beat the goalkeeper but Phillips tried to grab him by the feet. Kidd stumbled, then recovered, and put his shot into the side netting. But Burtenshaw had whistled for a penalty. Morgan scored.

Then the goal of the evening. It brought the whole of the stadium to its feet. In the 72nd minute Charlton put in one of his old familiar powerful shots, on the run, and thus gave United a 3-1 advantage with 10 men.

In the 88th minute Osgood scored a second goal for Chelsea after Dempsey's shot had been blocked.

Best's sending off was watched by Mr Eldon Griffiths, Minister for Sport. Mr Griffiths attended the match in view of recent comment on referees' "get tough" campaign.

The Irish international now faces the prospect of an extremely long suspension as he received a six weeks' suspended sentence in January of this year which will now automatically come into effect when he appears before the FA Disciplinary Committee.

When Best received his suspended sentence earlier this year he was also fined £250, the heaviest fine in British soccer history. In February Best again appeared before the Disciplinary Committee and successfully appealed against a caution during the match last

December in which Manchester City's Pardoe broke a leg.

Chelsea: Phillips; McCreadie, Boyie, Hollins, Dempsey, Harris, Smethurst, Hudson, Osgood, Baldwin, Houseman. **Sub**: Cooke.
Manchester United: Stepney; Fitzpatrick, Dunne, Gowling, James, Sadler, Morgan, Kidd, Charlton, Law, Best. **Sub**: Aston.
Referee: N. Burtenshaw (Great Yarmouth).

Guardian, 19 August 1971

GEORGE BEST: A CASE FOR CLEMENCY
John Samuel

No one at Crystal Palace on Saturday could have doubted that in George Best they were watching probably the finest forward in the world playing at the top of his form. The reality stood above the myth like a mountain jutting over the ground mists.

Yet today, as part of a policy to save professional football, an FA Disciplinary Committee will almost certainly remove this player from the game for a minimum of six weeks, and much longer if they choose to regard his punishment as exemplary.

The paradox is cruel and ludicrous. A refereeing purge primarily aimed at protecting cleverer, faster players from the calculated foul, has as its first victim the cleverest, fastest dribbler in the world. He appears following an incident at Chelsea in the first week of the season when he was cautioned for allegedly swearing at the referee, and he is already under a six-week suspended sentence.

These are an unhappy set of pressures for both the player and the disciplinary committee and it is as well to have the record completely straight. Best's three cautions before the Chelsea incident all occurred towards the end of last year: on 12 December, for a dangerous tackle on Pardoe of Manchester City; on 14 November for showing dissent while playing against Nottingham Forest; and on 17 October for showing dissent in the match against Leeds.

In the eight years he has been playing top football he has been sent off twice and severely disciplined for a third offence off the field. On 18 April 1970, he was sent off in the match between Northern Ireland and Scotland for throwing mud at the referee, Eric Jennings, but there was no punishment. On 3 December 1969, he knocked the ball from the hands of the referee, Jack Taylor – who also refereed at Crystal Palace on Saturday – as the players were leaving the field and he was suspended for four weeks and fined £100. On 16 October 1968, against Estudiantes, he was sent off for fighting and banned from two UEFA matches.

All Selhurst Park held its breath on Saturday when he was involved in another incident with Mr Taylor. This time he and McCormick collided, Mr Taylor ruled a foul by Best, though McCormick's rather clumsy efforts to win the ball initially may have seemed more culpable to some, and Best irritatedly backheeled the ball away after Palace had placed it for the free kick. Mr Taylor clearly deliberated with himself before settling for a short lecture.

Otherwise Best's behaviour was perfectly reasonable and his football at a level which tested mind and eye of opponents, spectators and, I have not the slightest doubt, referee. This, surely, is one of the reasons why the disciplinary committee and Best should cry truce today, and his punishment not exceed the six weeks hanging over him. If they choose to impose a heavy fine that is as maybe.

No one who has seen Best's bruised and battered body after some matches, or indeed the pictures, should be in much doubt of the provocation he has suffered. He cannot expect to escape hurt, because clumsier, slower players will simply catch him awkwardly from time to time.

To that extent he must show self control. On other occasions his own quickness will lead him into chancy tackles and fouls on his own account. He must still know how to accept decisions against himself. But he at least should know now that the refereeing intention, if not always the performance, is working his way.

Finally, soccer has to face the question whether it can afford to do without Best for most of the season when attendances are seriously declining, yet he is well capable of doubling a gate, as at Selhurst Park on Saturday.

Guardian, 13 September 1971

BEST ALLOWED TO PLAY ON
Albert Barham

George Best will not suffer a winter under suspension. In London yesterday he appealed against the decision of Norman Burtenshaw, the referee who sent him off the field during Manchester United's First Division match against Chelsea at Stamford Bridge on 18 August, and the FA Disciplinary Commission decided that his being dismissed was sufficient punishment.

They said they were not satisfied beyond reasonable doubt that Best directed his words at the referee. "They were foul and contrary to Rule 12," the commission stated afterwards, "and would call for stricter punishment in view of the referee's pre-match talk, when he warned players that he would send off players who used abusive language to him. In his evidence Mr Burtenshaw conceded this may have led players to think they could use it to other players."

The commission also decided that the existing

suspended sentence which has shadowed Best since January, when he was fined a record amount of £250 and given a suspended sentence of six weeks, should not be enforced.

Best spent almost 70 minutes before the commission, which was led by Vernon Stokes, a solicitor and chairman of the FA Disciplinary Committee, and made up of Len Shipman, president of the Football League, Stuart Jacobs, secretary of the Oxfordshire FA, and Lionel Smart, a former director of Bristol City. After deliberating for half an hour Best was then called back to be told the decision.

He was accompanied by Willie Morgan, the Manchester United outside right who had been cautioned immediately before Best was sent off, Frank O'Farrell, the United manager, and Cliff Lloyd, the secretary of the Professional Footballers' Association. The incident involving Best and Morgan occurred after Burtenshaw had allowed a Chelsea goal. Morgan protested, because it seemed that Osgood could have "climbed" on Gowling as he headed the ball. Best then joined in the argument. Though not in earshot, from what one saw of the incident, Best may consider himself fortunate that the commission dealt with him as they did.

The United party avoided meeting supporters and photographers at Euston by leaving the train at Watford and travelling the rest of the way by taxi. At a previous hearing Best had kept a disciplinary commission waiting for some two hours; yesterday he appeared exactly on time. He was ordered to pay the costs of the commission and his suspended sentence stands until next January. So he is available both for Manchester United and for Northern Ireland's European Championship matches, which begin with the game against the Soviet Union tomorrow week in Moscow.

Earlier yesterday Gordon Cumming of Reading and Alan Pinkney of Crystal Palace appealed against single cautions. They were told that, though the cautions would be recorded against them, because of the nature of the offences, they would not count towards the rule which requires players to come before the commission if they receive three in a year.

Well over 300 cautions have been administered this season. Until yesterday, players have been dealt with leniently by the commission, who realised that players could not have been aware of the authorities' decision to tighten discipline.

Yesterday's cases apart, the referees do need some indication from authority that their judgment will be backed up. Referees, like the football public, are not necessarily given the reason for any of the commission's decisions. As a public spectacle, the game has unquestionably improved through the curbing of petulance and the protection being given to the more skilful players. The authorities are no doubt hoping that the days of dwindling attendances are ending.

Obviously a situation must be avoided where authority seems to be facing both ways. Before the commission met yesterday the FA could have displayed a fine diplomacy by announcing an amnesty, saying they had made their point and it had been taken – and that this season's slate would now be wiped clean. But that moment has now passed. No one would have lost face. Now it is imperative that all connected with both the playing and administration must urgently meet and thrash out all their problems.

Guardian, 14 September 1971

GEORGE BEST, IN THE SHADOW OF THE GUNMEN
Hugh McIlvanney

Out on the fringes of Bramhall, just where Cheshire shakes off Manchester and takes its first confident lungfuls of country air, Jenny Lane takes you into Moor Lane and Moor Lane takes you into Blossoms Lane. Most days last week you could turn out of Blossoms Lane and, without warning, come up against the lunacy of Ulster. It was like finding a piece of shrapnel in your cornflakes.

Yet the connection between Bramhall and the Irish war is not as remote as it seems, for George Best lives in Blossoms Lane and George Best was born a Protestant on the outskirts of Belfast. The fact that the bigotries which assailed him in the streets and schools of his childhood never took hold on Best, never came near to drawing the kind of commitment that would have survived his 10 years in England, where orange and green are simply bright colours, all that is hardly relevant.

Birth and blood are irrevocable for Ulstermen now and the police cars that have been parked in Best's driveway at all hours of the day and night since last weekend were not there, as they have been in the past, because a young girl had hitch-hiked from Newquay to present her fantasies at his front door. The police were there last week because the footballer's life had been threatened in a way that obliged them to take the threats seriously.

Best was told he was going to be shot while playing for Manchester United at Newcastle a week ago and anxiety was increased when the team bus was broken into on the Friday night. He ate his meals in his hotel room, in the unsettling company of two detectives. Cranks have promised him all sorts of nasty treatment in the past but he does not pretend that he laughed off this latest prediction.

"I knew there were at least 40 policemen sent into the Newcastle ground because of the threat and I couldn't really get it out of my head that maybe this time the whole thing was real. I was definitely nervous for a while. I never stopped moving on the field. Somehow I felt that I should not stand still. Even when there was someone on the floor injured I kept running around. When I scored the goal I was hoping I might be taken off. That's how much it had got to me. I kidded the other players that it was the first time I had ever scored a goal without people coming over to congratulate me."

On the way back from Newcastle the Manchester United bus had an escort of two police cars. They were relieved in relays as county boundaries were crossed.

Then, last week, a woman in Alderley Edge, which is not far from Best's home, was badgered by two men who wanted his address and directions on how to get there. She reported that when she looked out of the window of her house after the men had left she thought she saw one of them with a gun. "It might have been a pipe or something like that," says Best. "The woman had been given a bit of a hard time by those characters and she was probably worked up. But anyway the police thought it was worth taking seriously and they have been round here every couple of hours or so to check up on the place."

Apart from the obvious lack of restraint among the extremists engaged in the Ulster conflict, the evidence that two men were menacing Best must have alarmed the police. Even if they were cranks they might have produced a mutual hysteria that would be much more dangerous than the individual madness of either of them.

This week Best's telephone has bleeped incessantly (he has an appliance in keeping with his uncompromisingly modern home and it does nothing as orthodox as ring) only to leave him with a sinister silence when he lifts the receiver. Much of the time he has turned the phone over to the answering device but this is something of a hardship because one of his main weapons against the loneliness that comes in through the glass walls and settles on the black leather furniture is to cradle the receiver and make jerky conversation, mainly with girls. He is not a natural on the phone, tending to offer monosyllabic, shorthand responses, but the peculiar intimate remoteness of these conversations helps to reconcile this shyness with his need for contact.

While I was with him last week his mother came on from Belfast. There is much more than a profound physical resemblance to make them close. His absence from home, and her knowledge of his special vulnerability, did sad damage to her health and he is worried that what is happening now may interrupt the recovery that has taken place over the last two years.

He replied to her inquiries coolly, with a muted flippancy, but when he came off he took his breath in sharply and shook his head. "My sister got shot in the leg coming out of a dance," he said. "Not badly, but bad enough. And she got shot because she was my sister.

"My family have been lucky that the trouble has not really got through to the housing estate where they live. At least, not to anything like the terrible extent that it has affected other parts of Belfast. But when I go home, or even when I speak to people over there, I can sense that attitudes are hardening. The Protestants are getting more Protestant and the Catholics more Catholic. It's horrible and there seems no way out of it."

Anyone who believes that Best's failure to play for Northern Ireland in Belfast a few weeks back was entirely due to injury is being unnecessarily naïve. He has been told that if he goes there he will never make it back to England. It is not a risk many of us would take in return for an international cap.

"Even the wildest rumours are believed over there. They're saying that I gave £3,000 to Ian Paisley to help finance one of his churches. Can you imagine anything more ridiculous? But that's the kind of rubbish that can get you shot."

He looks out through the glass into the fields around his £40,000 house. "If a sniper wanted to do a job on you he couldn't ask for a better place," he says. His laugh is more genuine than it might be.

It is a particularly painful irony that all this aggravation (his word) should come at a time when his career is going marvellously. He is playing to a new, almost incomprehensible peak, reaching out into areas of virtuosity that perhaps no other British player has ever explored. If Pelé really is in gentle decline then Best is conceivably the most gifted performer in the whole game of football.

"I think everything has improved. Frank O'Farrell must take a lot of the credit for what he has done at United, but I think his assistant, Malcolm Musgrove, is terrific too. Malcolm has us doing all sorts of things we never tried before – like making use of dead-ball situations. These used to be a joke with us. Now we score off them regularly.

"My own game has certainly developed because the team is doing well and I have the encouragement I need. I am strictly a front man now. They don't want me going back into my own half. Scoring goals, or at least having a hand in them, is what it has always been about for me, so I am going well. I think I am passing better than I ever did before, not more accurately because I thought I always struck the ball pretty well but at the right time. That's some difference."

One of the joys of talking to Best these days is that he has abandoned any attempt to be blasé about his feeling for football. "You know, I still find a special thrill in playing with goalposts that have nets. When we are training and there are no nets I feel like going in a huff and refusing to play. I still get a special charge when the ball makes that whirring noise as it hits the net."

Every great game he plays, and most of his performances turn out that way, increases his glamour and his earnings. He is paid about £12,000 a year from Manchester United and makes perhaps three times that from outside sources. The most spectacular of these is the George Best Annual. The initial print was 20,000 at £1. It sold out in three days and the sale has climbed to around 120,000.

"I used to joke that my ambition was to be a millionaire. Now it's not so much of a joke. I'll be disappointed if I'm not somewhere near it by the time I'm 30."

Then what? Restlessness is a natural condition in a man of 25 but in Best it may be a chronic affliction. "I've had Manchester. It's like Peyton Place. Everybody knows what everybody else is doing. I don't know if I could live anywhere in this country after I have finished. But I don't know where I want to go. I thought Switzerland was great but when I went there I found it was too perfect, too beautiful, just too much."

A friend of mine suggested that what Best needs is a woman. He means one woman instead of a thousand.

Observer, 31 October 1971

O'FARRELL'S FIRM LINE ON BEST
Eric Todd

George Best, who vanished from Old Trafford within a few days of signing to Manchester United as an apprentice 10 years ago, has again been posted missing. At least he has not been training all week, and as a result United's manager, Frank O'Farrell, has left him out of the squad for today's game against Wolverhampton Wanderers at Old Trafford. Beyond reporting his absence O'Farrell had nothing to say, except that Best would not be fit to play in the match.

Best said at his home in Bramhall last night that he had no comment to make on why he had failed to turn up for training during the week. His business agent,

Ken Stanley, said that Best had not been too well at the beginning of the week. He added: "It will all come out when he sees the boss, probably on Monday."

Whatever the cause of his absences, and whenever he may choose to go back to United, he could find O'Farrell in less sympathetic mood than was the father of the original prodigal son or, in more recent times, Sir Matt Busby when he was manager. Sir Matt has done as much as he could have been reasonably expected to do to keep Best in the straight and narrow path; the next meeting of Best and O'Farrell should be a rare test of O'Farrell's temper.

Best's form in recent weeks has been so far below its usual high standard that it has been obvious that all was not right with him. In a recent article in the *Daily Express* Best insisted that alleged escapades were figments of the imagination. He admitted that he was going through a lean spell as a player.

For all his genius Best has always been something of a problem on the field as well as off it. After a string of cautions between 1966 and 1968 he was sent off for the first time against Estudiantes at Old Trafford in March 1969, and was suspended for two matches by UEFA.

In December 1969 he was fined £100 and given a four weeks' suspension after knocking the ball out of the referee's hands at the end of a game at Maine Road. He was sent off again for throwing mud in the Northern Ireland v Scotland game at Belfast in April 1970, and sending off was considered sufficient punishment.

Three more cautions followed later that year and in January 1971 he was fined £250 and given a six weeks' suspended sentence. Previously he had missed a train to London and kept the disciplinary committee waiting for three hours.

Also in that January he was suspended by United for 14 days when he failed to catch the train for a match against Chelsea. He "went absent" in London for four days, before returning to Old Trafford with an apology. Last August he was sent off at Chelsea for arguing, but sending off was considered punishment enough. This season he has also been given police protection following alleged threats by the IRA.

Businessman, man about town and one of the wealthiest bachelors in the business, Best has to accept that he is the target for all and sundry who want to make capital out of his reputation, popularity, and skill. But unless he disciplines himself, or reacts more quickly to United's discipline, he can never hope to escape from the unsavoury limelight. And although he may yet achieve one of his objectives to be a millionaire by the time he is 30, he may have to seek an outlet other than football to build on the capital he already has.

Guardian, 8 January 1972

THE TEST OF O'FARRELL'S TEMPER
Albert Barham

George Best has been dropped from Manchester United's team. "He has not trained all the week and therefore is not fit to play against Wolverhampton Wanderers tomorrow," was the terse, official statement from Frank O'Farrell, the manager of United. He has not been seen at Old Trafford since they lost 0–3 to West Ham on Saturday at Upton Park.

Best's housekeeper had said he was not at home yesterday, but later in the day Best said he had been at home but had no comment to make. Earlier yesterday his friends appeared to have no knowledge of where he was staying. One of them, a business associate, Malcolm Mooney, said he had a drink with Best on Monday, but had not seen him since. "He looked a little peaky," he said, but thought he was worried about his recent form. He said he had not gone away with a girl friend.

His business agent, Ken Stanley, said yesterday that Best was not very well at the beginning of the week: "It will all come out when he sees the boss, probably on Monday," said Mr Stanley. Later, Stanley flew with Best to London.

He has been in Manchester United's team all season. Last week he wrote in a newspaper article: "I'm sick about the way I am playing. I'm going through one of those lean spells which can hit any player." That was also the view of O'Farrell at the weekend, but he added, "I have no complaints about George's attitude or the effort he puts into his training."

O'Farrell has been in Ireland and Scotland for much of the week on scouting missions and now faces, for the first time, a situation which stretched the patience of Sir Matt Busby when he was manager. It was exactly a year ago when Best had another week away from the club. He missed training, did not catch the train with the other players when they came to play Chelsea – and win 2-1 without him – on January 8 and subsequently spent part of his period away from the club at the home of the actress, Sinead Cusack, whose flat in Islington was under siege from the photographers and supporters. When he returned he apologised to Sir Matt and was said to have poured out all his personal and private problems to him. He was suspended by the club for two weeks.

Best has not been in trouble with the football authorities since August. He started the year with a record fine of £250 and in August was sent off the field for a remark he made to the referee. At a subsequent hearing it was decided that he should be cleared.

O'Farrell has said there has been no quarrel with Best. There seemed to be harmony in the club since O'Farrell's appointment and the same players who struggled last season have recaptured all their old form. But now O'Farrell faces his first public test in how he handles the temperaments of his star player.

Best's absence comes at a crucial time for the club. They have had their lead cut in the First Division to two points, and have only taken three from their past four matches. Today, at Old Trafford, Wolves create a club record by keeping the same team for 11 successive matches. They have not been beaten in 10 matches, eight in the League. Next week they play at Southampton in the FA Cup.

January cannot be poor Best's favourite month. In January 1970 he was suspended for 28 days and fined £100 by the FA for knocking the ball out of referee Jack Taylor's hands at the end of United's League Cup semi-final versus Manchester City. Exactly a year later he received a six weeks' suspended sentence and a record £250 fine from the FA after three bookings in 12 months. In the same month he was also suspended for 14 days by Manchester United after missing training and a train to London. And now come his latest January headlines.

Guardian, 8 January 1972

WHAT'S BEST FOR BEST?
Hugh McIlvanney

The first thing to be said about George Best's disappearance last week is that it was rather less than total. A moderately alert junior reporter could have been expected to find him in Manchester if only the newspapers had realised that they should have been looking for him.

It was not until Friday – when Manchester United announced their team for yesterday's match with Wolverhampton Wanderers, explaining the omission of Best with the information that he had not trained for a week and was therefore unfit for selection – that the problems at Old Trafford became public knowledge. That was when headline writers up and down the country reached for the verb to vanish.

If Best had indeed vanished his ghosted column in the *Daily Express* on Friday would have been even more ghostly than it was. In fact, the *Express* man who interviews him to produce the weekly piece, John Roberts, had talked to him in the usual way.

Roberts went back to the player's house in Blossoms Lane, Bramhall, in Cheshire, on Friday but found Best unwilling to come out of his bedroom. A plaintive reminder by Ken Stanley, Best's agent, that he had a contract with the *Daily Express*, had no effect, which was hardly surprising when one considers that his more important contract with Manchester United had not drawn him out of his remoteness.

Best said he intended to speak to no one about his situation until he faced Frank O'Farrell, the Manchester United manager, on Monday. As soon as Stanley left the bedroom, the door was slammed and locked.

Roberts, assuming that his quarry had holed up for the night, went to his own home nearby to file a story. While he was away, Best apparently went to Manchester airport and booked a ticket to London. At Heathrow he was picked up by a Rolls-Royce and, in the marvellously inevitable phrase of the reporters who failed to keep up with him, "whisked away into the night towards the M4".

But still there was to be no really convincing vanishing act. The Irish footballer arrived, complete with velvet jacket and Miss Great Britain, Carolyn Moore, at Tramp, a discotheque in the West End of London. He was on hand early yesterday morning in the doorway of the club, at 40 Jermyn Street, when a group of his friends were involved in a scuffle with a photographer.

The photographer, Graham Wood, emerged from the incident with a sore jaw, but Best had nothing to do with that. Throughout the melee he had his arm around Miss Moore, who appeared at Olympia in London later yesterday to promote an ice-cream product and deny suggestions that she was about to marry Best.

Miss Moore, who is 19, clearly regarded Best's further disappearance as highly partial. "I expect him to get in touch with me during the day," she said.

Another who was hoping for contact was Frank O'Farrell, who issued a statement which had to be interpreted as distinctly conciliatory. "I would like George to put whatever has been troubling him behind him and resume training as soon as possible in preparation for our Cup tie with Southampton next Saturday," he said.

O'Farrell's reaction is marked by the same tolerance as was shown by Sir Matt Busby a year ago when he had to discipline Best after the Irishman had absented himself and turned up at the London flat of Sinead Cusack, the actress.

The manager admits having discussed Best's recent disappointing form with the player but insists that what he said did not amount to a dressing down – although one of their conversations concerned a letter that alleged Best had been seen coming out of a night club at five o'clock on the morning before a match. Best dismissed the accusation as ludicrous.

In all the overblown confusion of the episode, what seems unquestionable is that there has been an erosion, however temporary, of the trust between the manager and his greatest player. O'Farrell was given to understand that Best had been in Belfast during the past week seeing his family about a domestic problem (his mother has suffered bouts of illness) but discovered first hand that this was not true.

If Best did not vanish last week, a disturbing amount of the public's affection for him did. As a very special talent, arguably the most special British football has ever produced, he is entitled to unusual behaviour from time to time and his defenders will say that one blow-out per year is a small price to pay for the unique entertainment he provides for millions of us.

But even after allowing for the traditional licence given to genius, for the smothering pressures created by being a Belfast schoolboy one day and a superstar the next, for the disorientating effects of personalised adulation on a scale that British sport has never known before, for the worry caused by concern about a troubled family in troubled Ulster and threats on his own life, even after allowing for all this many of those closest to him think it is time for the soft handling of Best to stop.

Perhaps they are wrong. Perhaps his emotional condition requires not harsh discipline but treatment. Either way, it is obvious that he cannot go on operating effectively as a great professional footballer if his behaviour is going to become increasingly unreliable and irresponsible.

If a star of the theatre abruptly walks out on a successful show the public and his fellow actors are not quick to forgive him. If he repeats the offence, their response is bound to be bitter.

Even in those pubs where football is granted an almost cosmic significance the talk of Best last week was exasperated or cynical. "Who gives a monkey's where he is?" "Manchester United have a number for him but when they ring it God keeps answering." "They're going to let him go and sign somebody less temperamental, like Greta Garbo."

A less frivolous comment came from a senior United player. "Don't waste too much sympathy on Georgie. What he needs is a kick up the arse. And you know what I think of the wee man." I do. He loves Best like a wayward brother.

Observer, 9 January 1972

O'FARRELL AWAITS A CONTRITE BEST
Albert Barham

Frank O'Farrell, manager of Manchester United, has made conciliatory noises to nudge the errant George Best back to Old Trafford today for a full week's training before an FA Cup match as important as the League match the player missed. "Forget your troubles; come and join us," has been the theme.

The cost of a week without training, without communication with the club, of omission from the team, and of a Friday night on which Best lived it up in London, has still to be counted. Today he is due to see O'Farrell and to train with his colleagues. Most of them remember a year ago, when somewhat similar circumstances prevailed.

But while they pondered on the fateful match against Wolves on Saturday, Best danced with Miss Great Britain in a London discotheque until 4 a.m. While the sourness of defeat was still upon them Best ate well in Knightsbridge before returning to his home in Bramhall.

It is one thing to be the gay bachelor with a bevy of girlfriends; it is another when colleagues have to suffer. There is a feeling that some would like to do without him. One feels that some more serious attempt to reform is required of Best than an apology to his colleagues, particularly, one to O'Farrell. That will not be enough this time.

O'Farrell is well enough placed in the club to severely discipline Best. So far he has suggested only a chat, so that Best can offer a reason for his action. The manager has the Cup match on Saturday at Southampton to consider, especially now that United have reached a bad patch in the League. It was at Southampton on 27 November that Best scored three of United's five goals. He has not scored since. O'Farrell has the task of trying to get Best on a path which no one has yet been able to make him follow.

The manager will give a sympathetic ear to anything Best tells him, either in the nature of a confidential chat about his problems, or an explanation for his absence and his attitude. That is his job. But United, though they may accept a heavy tax on their patience, are not slow to remind errant players that no one is greater than the club. Denis Law was made available for transfer by manager Sir Matt Busby when he stepped out of line.

Sir Matt "didn't dish out the toffees when he called a player into the office," one player, no longer young, remembers.

O'Farrell, who had told his friends how Best had been a model player since he took control at Old Trafford in the summer, has an engaging smile, a soft Cork brogue; but he can be uncommonly hard. He will not put Best on transfer.

Meanwhile, O'Farrell hopes that Best is prepared to say he is sorry, and make a fresh start.

Guardian, 10 January 1972

BEST'S PENALTY – CONFINED TO DIGS
Sports Staff

Manchester United has tempered justice with a fair amount of mercy in dealing with George Best, its 25-year-old star player who went absent without leave last week.

The club's manager, Mr Frank O'Farrell, said in a prepared statement at Old Trafford yesterday: "George Best came back to see me this morning, and we had a very frank talk with one another. His absence from training was a very serious breach of his contract. He would have been suspended, but it would not have been in the best interests of the club.

"He has been fined two weeks' salary, and he will be required to train every morning and afternoon this week in preparation for Saturday's Cup tie at Old Trafford. He will also have to train the next five times the players have a day off. He will be required to live in lodgings until the end of the season, when the position will be reviewed. He will then be under supervision when he is away from home."

Questions to Mr O'Farrell then elicited the further information that:

1. Best had given an explanation for his absence, and had expressed his regrets;

2. Best had put forward his various problems, none of which was specified, and had admitted that his life was "complicated";

3. The other United players were very disappointed with Best's behaviour last week;

4. There is no question of Best leaving United, and he does not want to;

5. The matter of Best's contract was not mentioned, and no issue of pay was raised; and

6. Sir Matt Busby was not consulted. "It has nothing to do with him," Mr O'Farrell said.

"Best obviously has problems," Mr O'Farrell said. "But instead of sharing them, he tends to opt out. It will be in his own interests to have someone to go home to."

George Best arrived at Manchester United's training ground in Lower Broughton Road at noon, and went straight into the gymnasium, accompanied by Malcolm Musgrove, United's senior coach, Pat Crerand, and several junior players.

"The boss has said all there is to be said: George has no comment to make," Mr Musgrove said.

Best is expected to go back to his former landlady, Mrs Mary Fullaway, at her council house in Aycliffe Road, Chorlton-cum-Hardy, a Manchester suburb. He had lived there from the age of 15, when he joined

United, until he moved into his own £30,000 house at Bramhall, Cheshire, last year. Mrs Fullaway said last night that Mr Best would be "very welcome" to return to his digs.

"I will be delighted to see George again," she said. "He came to us at Christmas, and he is almost regarded as part of the family." Mr Best has continued to pay rent for the room there.

The fine of two weeks' salary will cost the United player about £400.

His girl friend, Miss Caroline Moore, aged 19, the present Miss Great Britain, whom he took to dinner and a discotheque in London on Friday evening, said last night that she was worried about him moving back to digs. "But in a way I am glad for George, as I think he was often lonely in that large house," she said. "I really expected something like this, and I think George did too."

Guardian, 11 January 1972

BEST IS HOME AND AWAY
Eric Todd

Frank O'Farrell, Manchester United's manager, has proved himself to be more of a psychologist than a strict disciplinarian. And George Best could be all the better for it.

Those of us who suggested that Best should be suspended or similarly degraded after absenting himself without leave last week have been routed by O'Farrell, who has decided in his wisdom that the player is greater than the team, problem or no problem, loss of form or no loss of form. Best accordingly has been kept on the strength, and therefore will be available for Saturday's FA Challenge Cup tie at Southampton after doing a double training stint this week. If he scores six goals as he did against Northampton Town after completing his month's suspension two seasons ago, United's supporters at least will be prepared to forget as well as to forgive.

Inevitably, perhaps, there will be some people, not excluding a few of his colleagues, who will feel that Best has escaped lightly. The loss of two weeks' wages certainly will mean very little to a man reportedly worth many thousands. And what punishment, physical at any rate, is there in extra training? On the other hand, those additional stints in isolation will afford Best plenty of time for reflection and self-recrimination, plenty of time on which to ponder on the disadvantages of that loneliness which by all accounts has been one of his major problems.

It is hard to believe, nevertheless, that a man of Best's personality and money need ever be alone. Perhaps in his isolation he will reflect on the desirability of finding different company, different pursuits and hobbies, and above all of finding somebody reliable and understanding to help him with his problems. Like a good wife, for instance.

The biggest blow to his pride, however, may be the transition from a luxury house to more modern "digs" which at least will provide him with every mod. con. and every home comfort such as he had before he plunged rather prematurely into Manchester's green belt. It may be, of course, that Best will start worrying about what is to happen to the house in Bramhall in his absence, but United no doubt will take care of that without giving it to the National Trust.

Best has had enough advice these past few days to last himself a lifetime. Mixed-up kid he is, but the fact remains that he broke the terms of his contract and deserved to be punished. He has expressed his regret, and no useful purpose would be served therefore by labouring on this or any other point. It is unfortunate and it is quite inevitable that a player of Best's genius should be subjected to more pressures than the rest. It is no less unfortunate that he has shown few signs of being able to cope with those pressures. Whether he is to blame entirely is a matter for conjecture.

This much is certain. In the interests of Best, of Manchester United, and of football everywhere, the sooner he can sort himself out (or be sorted out in the kinder sense of the expression) the better. It would help, too, if everybody tried to treat him more as a human being instead of some sort of idol or a freak in a sideshow, and took away some of the seamy limelight from him and his activities off the field.

We all respect George Best as a footballer. Some of us are sick and tired of hearing and reading about his private life.

Guardian, 11 January 1972

WHAT DOES O'FARRELL DO NOW?
Eric Todd

Frank O'Farrell this week could strike a decisive blow on behalf of football discipline by suspending George Best or playing him in the reserve side for a month. Should the Manchester United manager ignore the opportunity, then the game can resign itself to continued anarchy and to the continued realisation that the players and not the managers are running their clubs.

There is however a gleam of hope in O'Farrell's request to Best to come home – without the usual rider, "All is forgiven." Whatever else O'Farrell may forgive, Best's attitude would not be tolerated in any other walk of life, and there is no reason why a footballer should be given special dispensation.

But is Best entirely to blame?

It would appear that he is not equipped temperamentally to deal with his genius, not proof against those who may seek to use him. In short, he should have been taken in hand years ago.

In September 1965 Best, on his own admission, was "living 24 hours a day, attending dances which seldom finished before midnight, and then on to parties which generally went on until the next day." Matt Busby left him out of the team for three matches because he didn't think Best's mind was on football. "I was only annoyed because I had been found out," said Best. There's an admission for you. In January last year Matt Busby suspended Best for two weeks after going AWOL, and still Best has not learnt his lesson.

Of course Best is a genius. So was Hughie Gallacher and we all know what happened to him. Roy Paul was another who crashed from the heights because he did the wrong things with the wrong people at the wrong time.

The theatre, the films and the world of literature are full of instances of men and women who made mistakes which reduced their careers and bank balances to ruins. Best at 26 would do well to consider the fallen, and take care that he does not find himself numbered among them.

One can sympathise with O'Farrell, and with all the managers who have players of outstanding football qualities, not so much because of their worth on the field, but because their very presence, home and away, can add a few thousands to the attendances.

Therein lies one of the tragedies of genius. It means automatic selection as often as not no matter if form be good or bad.

But the public can be fickle and as one genius drops out the popular side sooner or later will find another favourite. O'Farrell should dwell on that when he comes to take Best to task. He must also consider the rest of his players. Best is not indispensable, and if I were O'Farrell – I am grateful I am not – I would make one final effort to bring Best to heel by putting him in the reserve side, and making him earn his place on the first team. If Best does not accept the challenge, then he is no use to United or to anybody else.

I believe that many people are tired of Best and his tantrums. I believe too that many people wish that he would get married and put us all out of our misery and speculation. Then he could get on with the job for which he is not badly paid. If he wants as much money as he believes Bobby Charlton is getting, then let him behave like Charlton off the field, as well as on it.

Guardian, 12 January 1972

UNITED PULL AWAY IN EXTRA TIME
Eric Todd

Manchester United: 4
Southampton: 1

Manchester United gave Southampton a goal start and a beating by 4-1 in extra time in their FA Challenge Cup third round replay last night in the presence of 50,966 spectators. It was a triumph for George Best and for perseverance and earned United a visit to Preston North End in the next round.

United were made to work hard for their first victory since Nottingham Forest were at Old Trafford on 4 December. Or it might be nearer the truth to say that they made it hard for themselves, especially in the first half when the whole forward line looked in need of shooting practice. Charlton himself gave plenty of opportunities for fielding to the Stretford enders who were chanting "Give us a goal."

Once they had equalised, however, United were much more like their old, better known, selves. Yet they were still below perfection in defence where hesitation and occasional confusion prevent the side from being what they used to be. But it would be uncharitable to be hypercritical of any team which can recover from being a goal down and then win by such a convincing margin. United might well have had vivid memories of their European Cup final against Benfica when that fourth goal went in.

It is gratifying to be able to write again about Best as a footballer. Whatever his domestic problems he showed no sign of external pressures last night, not even from Southampton. He was impudent and he was brilliant. He was unselfish and he was incomparable. He scored two goals and would have made many more if his colleagues had always been as sharp as he was.

Morgan, who gets less of the limelight, nevertheless played a conspicuous part in the victory and young McIlroy, until he was withdrawn in favour of Aston, gave a good account of himself. In defence O'Neil did exceptionally well and went close to scoring in the closing minutes while Stepney saved United more than once during Southampton's period of mastery.

Southampton wilted under United's final onslaught but before it they made a generous contribution to a hard-fought, entertaining match. Paine was as near irrepressible as made no difference and his wicked centres allied to Davies's reception of them were a source of constant anxiety to Edwards and company. Channon, always, was in the thick of things – he and Fry were booked for over-zealous tackles as, later, was Gowling for time wasting – and he had worked himself to a standstill when he gave way to Kirkup in extra time.

In defence, Stokes and Gabriel were outstanding and Martin made one or two good saves when United at last got down to business. And none of them was better than that he brought off when O'Brien passed the ball back to him hurriedly and carelessly. But Southampton were well beaten in the end by a United side which had determination stamped all over it.

Southampton took the lead in the 22nd minute. A superb pass by O'Brien reached Paine, who centred it with his customary accuracy, and Channon's head did the rest. Stepney got his hands to the ball but could not prevent it from entering the net.

United came back and Law hit the crossbar with a fine header. And they kept at it and Best equalised in the 68th minute with a brilliant individual goal with his left foot.

In the last minute of normal time Martin saved brilliantly from Morgan but in the 96th minute Sadler hooked the ball past him from close in. Southampton had very little to offer after that and Best scored his second in the 115th minute, and three minutes later Aston prodded home the fourth.

Manchester United: Stepney; O'Neil, Burns, Gowling, Edwards, Sadler, Morgan, McIlroy, Charlton, Law, Best.
Southampton: Martin; McCarthy, Fry, Stokes, Gabriel, Byrne, Paine, Channon, Davies, O'Brien, Jenkins.
Referee: K. E. Walker (Ashford).

Guardian, 20 January 1972

TOP OF HIS NEW CLASS
John Arlott

It is customary to speak of George Best as unique; and in terms of playing ability – and sometimes of behaviour – the description is accurate. In another and probably more important respect, he represents a socially important group. He is the first British "millionaire" footballer – able to build himself an expensive house and drive a Bentley – a type formerly unknown in this country but shortly to become a relatively familiar figure.

It was only in 1961 that the maximum wage for English footballers was abolished. Legally speaking it did not exist in Scotland – as became effectively apparent when Billy Steel pressed for a transfer from Derby County to Dundee in 1950. That fact, however, has not yet produced a situation there comparable with that of, for instance, Best and Bobby Moore here.

It is now possible for an outstanding player in England to earn as much as £7,000 by playing football alone; while perfectly legitimate, perhaps even desirable, transfers can produce capital gains running into four figures: outside income can be as large as his businesses can provide or his managers contrive.

Jimmy Greaves enjoyed half his playing career under the new dispensation and derived a fair proportion of its benefits. No major performer, however, has yet spent his entire playing life on an unlimited salary. The footballers who were 17 when the fresh situation was created are now only 26 years old, with some years of effective life still ahead of them.

It does not need the appearance of formerly outstanding international players from the dockyards in neckerchiefs or from street newspaper stalls or unskilled labouring, to emphasise what little guarantee a successful football career offers of continuing prosperity. Outstanding talent is apparent so early that the player who possesses it is almost certain to be taken directly from school on to the staff of a club. One of such ability is likely to be single-minded about the game and, especially when those involved in international or club tours or competitions have barely time for a family holiday between the end of one season and the start of training for the next, there is little opportunity of adequate preparation for a subsequent career.

For almost a century football has deposited the men it has used on the labour market at between 30 and 40; the better the player the more dangerously late his "dumping" is likely to be.

It is unusual to find a man outstanding – in many of these instances it is not inaccurate to say a genius – in a particular walk of life capable of achieving equal standing, or making an equal income, in a second undertaking.

This must be especially true where the first activity is physical. A period in a lower league may stave off the final day for the professional footballer but eventually he must turn to another form of livelihood. Some stay in the game; but only a few can be managers and that is as insecure a calling as any in the country. Some become trainers, masseurs or coaches, but they are a minority.

The modern game contains its graduates – such as Gowling, Heighway and Hall – with a profession to hand when football no longer needs them: but their kind will always be the exception who prove the rule.

For most the game is not only a living but a life. It is said that the cricketers summoned from the pit in the 19th century to play for Nottinghamshire were at pains, out of season, to go at midday in their best, heavy, grey, tweed suits and sit drinking outside the local pub where the outgoing and returning shifts of pitmen would see them and recognise the extent of their success. The living was also the life.

The retired footballer, like any other performer, misses his status, his local fame and his newspaper headlines, which must make the transition to a less happy financial state the more bitter.

The Professional Footballers' Association has been farseeing and capable in arranging a pension scheme for its members: and many clubs have been cooperative. Thus a currently regular first-team player for Arsenal can expect a pension of about £1,500 at the age of 35 –

a vastly comforting provision for the present-day footballer by comparison with his empty-handed predecessor of only a few years ago.

In some ways the run-of-the-mill player may almost be best off, especially this is so if he recognises his ordinariness early and makes the most of his pleasure, local celebrity and income, without staying too long in the game. He will make his preparations for another living early, and his pension will seem a kind of bonus.

For the better player, pension notwithstanding a gap will remain. The man accustomed to £120 a week cannot maintain his established standard on £30; and this gap is important. As a well-known international remarked recently – "In the twenty-pound-a-week days you knew that when you finished you only had to earn £20 to stay level: but £5,000 a year is a different matter: that is not easy to make. I am trying to build a business that will bring it in – but it is not easy for a man whose only training is as a footballer."

The outstanding player – good enough say, to win a few international caps – granted an average career, married and accepting his responsibilities, should not find it difficult to save and invest thoroughly enough for subsequent work and his pension to keep him in relative comfort.

For the peak player, of the Best type, whose income may be several times that even of his colleagues in a national team, the problems are different. The rewards of what is called stardom – especially the extra-professional rewards – can be extremely high but are rarely enduring. These activities plus the football which gives rise to them are sufficient to keep most young men fully occupied. With too little time to handle their own affairs, and generally slight experience of the methods or the financial standards of these alien worlds, they must entrust their future security not merely to the immediate acumen but the far-sightedness and integrity of business agents or managers.

For Best, who lives an important part of his life at second-hand, realities must often become confused with the unknown. Bewildering as that problem may be, many would be happy to stand in his shoes – or boots.

Guardian, 21 January 1972

OLD PALS ACT ALREADY
Paul Wilcox

Manchester United: 2
Huddersfield Town: 0

Manchester United's bright new future supposedly began on Saturday with their first League win since 4 December. But perhaps a more realistic assessment of whether their outlay on Moore and Buchan will revitalise their sagging spirits sufficiently to hide their continuing lack of control in midfield should be deferred until they meet a team who, unlike Huddersfield Town, are not having to come to terms with mediocrity.

Not to put too much of a damper on things, however, United's recent acquisitions ensured a performance which while still patchy was a vast improvement on their recent efforts. If anything, and in spite of Moore's goal, the more rewarding individual presence was Buchan's.

From all accounts Best finds in Moore a kindred spirit, a man within the club with whom he can identify. In short, a friend on the field as well as off it. Hopefully, not to be patronising, Moore is what Best has needed for some time, and if so £200,000-plus is a cheap price to pay for someone of known quality who can bring out the genius of another.

Best and Moore struck a quick bond. That Best

wanted to create a goal for the new boy was obvious and he dragged Town's defence out of position and engineered chances so that it was almost inevitable that Moore's first appearance for United should have the bonus of a goal. But more important, Best's renewed and imaginative contribution to the attack also found him remembering how to turn mercurially and how to shoot with devastating power, as he did after 37 minutes to score the first goal, the ball going in off a post, and after 61 minutes when Moore set up Best for a stinging drive which David Lawson could only palm upwards. Moore headed simply into the empty net and the mutual admiration society had reached its height.

Manchester United: Stepney; O'Neil, Dunne, Buchan, James, Sadler, Morgan, Kidd, Charlton, Best, Moore.
Huddersfield Town: D. Lawson; Clarke, Hutt, S. Smith, Ellam, Cherry, D. Smith, Dolan, Worthington, J. Lawson, Chapman. **Sub**: Jones.
Referee: G. W. Hill (Kirby Muxloe).

Guardian, 13 March 1972

GEORGE BEST IS TAKEN TO MODEST TASK
Eric Todd

The FA's Rule 27 (section c) which strays towards compassion again has stood George Best in good stead. For his most recent breaches of contract – opting out of Manchester United's match at Tel-Aviv, and writing unvetted newspaper articles – he has been suspended for two weeks without pay from next Monday, the maximum penalty specified in the above rule. He will miss United's preseason tour which takes in Torquay, Bournemouth, Copenhagen, and West Berlin.

In addition, United have accepted an offer from Pat

Crerand, United's youth team coach, to have Best as a lodger, so that in the words of Frank O'Farrell, United's manager, Best can "establish regular sleeping and living habits which we feel will give him support in the early stages." The early stages, that is to say, of his rehabilitation and restitution.

O'Farrell, who informed the player of United's verdict before announcing it at the informal press conference at Old Trafford, made it clear that Best had made the initial approach, had expressed contrition, and had renewed his desire to continue playing for United. In view of the FA rule and Best's value to the team when he was in the mood, O'Farrell scarcely could have taken any other step. It was noticeable, however, that when asked if this were Best's last chance, O'Farrell settled for a wistful smile and "You know me. An eternal optimist."

This was the fourth time since 1965 that Best had been on the domestic carpet, and the third since January last year. In January this year he was fined two weeks' salary, but was not suspended because "it was not in the best interests of the club." He was also ordered to leave his luxury home in Bramhall and go into private lodgings, but this experiment was not a success. O'Farrell's observations yesterday had a familiar ring.

It remains to be seen whether Crerand, now one of United's elder and respected statesmen, and his wife can succeed where one landlady at least and United themselves have failed. The Crerands have made a brave and magnanimous gesture, and it is to be hoped that they do not regret it when the idolisers queue up outside their home hoping for a glimpse of United's wayward genius.

Best in my view is a very fortunate man not only because he has a patient manager and tolerant colleagues, but because he is still a United player. If he be truly penitent and subscribes more readily to the requirements of discipline off the field as well as on it, he will not lack for genuine help and encouragement. He cannot, however, expect too many last chances. Old Trafford is running low in fatted calves.

Guardian, 22 July 1972

BEST DROPPED TO AWAIT SHOWDOWN
Albert Barham

George Best will appear before the board of directors of Manchester United next week to explain his absence from training. He has been dropped from the team which tomorrow plays at Norwich. He has been fined three days' pay. He has been served with a summons following an incident in a night club in which a Salford girl claimed she was struck in the face. Best's appearance before the directors could be the final showdown in the strangely tolerant attitude the club have taken towards the often wayward player. He faces disciplinary action by the club for the fifth time in less than two years.

The questions being asked are whether the rift between player and club is now irrevocable; and, if so, will Manchester United make Best available for transfer.

Best may hope that his actions in breaching club discipline will bring him nearer to getting a move to a London club. With the Common Market in sight early next year, it is possible that, if free movement of players is allowed, Best could join a European club. His best form often attracts some 5,000 more spectators to a match, though, through his temperament, he needs strong control.

Best arrived an hour late at the United training centre in Salford yesterday. It is understood he had been with his solicitors at a meeting in the city centre. He remained half an hour, then drove off in his E-type Jaguar. He would make no comment. Frank O'Farrell, the manager, followed soon afterwards. He wound down the window of his car to announce that Best was dropped, and that he would appear when next the directors met.

Unless Best can give an acceptable explanation to the directors next week he can expect severe punishment. These recurring lapses do little to improve harmony among the other players or the spirit of the club now having to fight to survive in the First Division.

In January 1971 Best was suspended for two weeks for a breach of training regulations. In January 1972 he was dropped for the match against Wolves. He had come to London and missed training for a week. He was subsequently fined two weeks' wages, told to move from his £30,000 home into lodgings, and ordered extra training. Best promised to make "a genuine attempt to make amends."

Instead of playing for Northern Ireland in the home internationals, and for Manchester United in their pre-season match in Israel, Best went to Spain. He then put his name to a lucrative article stating that he had quit football. Later he changed his mind and apologised to the club. He was fined and suspended from the club's other pre-season matches.

He is already under suspension for three Northern Ireland matches by FIFA, having been sent off against Bulgaria.

Although United have been struggling to find form since the start of the season, Best had been playing reasonably well until recent weeks. Then he began missing training, and the incidents this week must surely put his career with the club in jeopardy.

Guardian, 1 December 1972

UNITED FEEL ENOUGH IS BEST
Eric Todd

Manchester United at last have decided that the club is greater than the individual, and have put George Best on the transfer list. After a full meeting of the board at Old Trafford yesterday, Frank O'Farrell, United's manager, issued the following statement:

"After careful consideration, the board and manager of Manchester United Football Club have decided that they have no alternative but to place George Best on the transfer list. Clubs will be notified in due course."

The board's findings were delivered to Best's lodgings in Chorlton. Best was not at home, nor did he attend the board meeting – "We don't know where he is," said O'Farrell – although if he had not missed training on Monday and again yesterday, he would have been ordered to attend.

So ends, predictably, another chapter in the history of one of the most colourful, talented, and controversial characters in the history of football. The next chapter is a matter for conjecture, and it will be interesting to see which club is prepared to take a chance and try to succeed where Manchester United, in spite of every effort, obviously have failed.

There is no doubt at all that United will not entertain any offer below £350,000 – they may even ask for one or two players as part of the deal – and it is possible that he will finish up with a foreign club. More than one British player has fallen for the lucrative inducements of South American football. More than one has returned home disillusioned, and Best is in no mental state to stand any more disillusionment or frustration.

First Sir Matt Busby, then Wilf McGuinness, and finally O'Farrell were tolerance itself, but Best was not always ready to share his problems. He was contrite enough when he was disciplined, but it was not long before he was off the rails again. He has shown a complete disregard for discipline, and several times he has been suspended and fined by his club for missing training sessions. On the field he has been brilliant and antagonistic, and more than once has been sent off, and suspended. Nothing and nobody, as they say, could do anything with him.

He entered business with some success based on his reputation as a footballer. He has frequented the night spots and once or twice has been involved in "scuffles". Next month he has to answer a summons for assault, but United have made it clear that this had no bearing on their decision.

Whether Sir Matt Busby was too lenient in Best's formative years is a matter of opinion. O'Farrell certainly has done his best to bring his wayward genius to some sort of rational behaviour. But there seemed to be as much relief as there was disappointment when he made his announcement.

"We must consider the future of the club, and the morale of the other players. We have done all we could with Best but we have not been as successful as we could have wished. He has not behaved like a full-time professional at all."

Incidentally, Best almost certainly will be entitled to five per cent of whatever transfer fee is involved because he did not ask for a move. Nor would United legally be justified in withholding that share because of his indiscipline, for which he has been punished already.

Guardian, 6 December 1972

THE CASE FOR GEORGE BEST – FOOTBALLER
David Lacey

The scene was an eve of match press reception in the offices of the *Belfast Telegraph* five years ago. The following day Northern Ireland were due to play Scotland in a home international at Windsor Park, and, not surprisingly, the main topic of conversation concerned the chances of an Irish victory, or, rather, the possibility of George Best inspiring an Irish victory.

Pessimism was rife. Best, it was said, seldom put himself out for his country; he was not the player for Ireland that he was for Manchester United; he might produce some touches of skill, but Ireland would be unwise to rely on him.

Whatever might have been Irish intentions in that match, the matter was taken out of their hands by the subject of the previous evening's discussion, for Best destroyed the Scots with what is still the most exciting display of individual skill that one has seen before or since. On a thickly grassed, heavy pitch he took on clutches of defenders singlehanded, burrowing into their midst and leaving them stranded with a swerve here, a wiggle there, and mesmeric ball control. Once or twice his green shirt was almost lost to view as the dark blue of the Scottish defenders crowded round him, the ball catapulting out of the thicket of players as Best still managed to get in a shot.

Northern Ireland scored the only goal of the match, created by Best's pass. Near the end of the game he set off on an ambitious course from near the halfway line, leaving Tommy Gemmell flat on his back as he sold him a double dummy, and he dribbled through the entire Scottish defence before, anticlimactically, planting the ball wide. Obviously, some watched Len Shackleton perform similar feats; indeed, one saw Jimmy Greaves do this for Tottenham, and he scored, but Best's dribble was merely the climax to a wonderful performance, the key with which one can unlock memories of the match as a whole.

Memories are a precious personal possession for a follower of football. They can be challenged and criticised, but they cannot be denied or altered, and it would be cheering to think that this week, with Best's football career apparently taking another downward spiral, there are those who remain grateful for the exhilarating entertainment he has provided over the last eight years, and who will remember this when the headlines and the gossip have been forgotten.

Over the years one has been told more than once that "United would be better off without him" or, more recently, "football would be better off without him." Neither statement bears close analysis. When all his problems, both on and off the field, are weighed against him, Best still has been good for Old Trafford in particular and football in general. A sports writer has professed, twice this week, that he finds Best a bore and the secretary of the Football League has been quoted as saying that he is fed up with hearing about him. One can only point out that there are many thousands of people who, for a brief while on a Saturday afternoon or week-day evening, have become less bored and less fed up through watching Best play, and it is a fair assumption that if ever he leaves Manchester United his next club can expect a dramatic rise in their gate receipts.

For George Best remains a saleable commodity. Of course any manager signing him would be gambling with the harmony of his team – as did Malcolm Allison when he brought Rodney Marsh into the Manchester City side last season – but the fact that a number of leading clubs became interested the moment Best was placed on the transfer list is proof of his lasting value as an entertainer.

The record attendance at St James' Park, Newcastle, is the 68,586 who watched a First Division match against Chelsea in 1930. The main attraction that day was the Chelsea centre forward, Hughie Gallacher, who had just been transferred to the London club from Tyneside for the then staggering fee of £10,000. Chelsea are the most strongly tipped of the London clubs to buy Best, and there is an obvious though superficial parallel with Gallacher, who had a brilliant career with Newcastle but was frequently at odds with his club.

He was never the player at Stamford Bridge that he had been at Newcastle, and after finishing with football, with his home life disintegrating, he took to drink and eventually committed suicide by throwing himself under an express train. By comparison Best's life so far has been a sea of sober tranquillity. But doubtless there were those who, on hearing of Gallacher's end, still preferred to remember the little Scot for his football, his goals for Newcastle, and his outstanding games for the Scotland of James, Morton and Jackson.

That, one is sure, is how Best will be remembered by the ordinary supporter, and while his off-the-field activities will continue to make the bigger headlines, it is by the smaller print that his contribution to the history of the game as an entertainment ought to be judged.

Guardian, 8 December 1972

THE LONER
Arthur Hopcraft

It is a matter of common regret among photographers who specialise in sport that George Best seldom makes good action pictures for them. The reason is that, unlike Bobby Charlton or Denis Law or Brazil's Pelé or Italy's Riva, there is nothing exaggerated in any of Best's movements on the football field. There is none of the strut and swagger of Law, although Best is as combative and can head goals as improbably; none of the majesty of Charlton, although Best can kick goals as powerfully.

No other player in Europe, and only Pelé in the world, has excited crowds as much as Best has; and he is equally thrilling on the television screen, because the film camera can encompass his intricacy and the scope of his play as the human eye can. But when the moment of action is frozen, the man hardly ever appears stretched or to be straining, or even urging. This is instructive about Best. There is something in his personality, in total contrast to the image of flamboyant irresponsibility that has grown in the public mind, that makes him naturally conceal himself. Just as he hides intention on the field he is secretive off it. He is an intensely private person.

Here is the paradox. The media hunt him. Best is seen so often, in newspaper and magazine pictures, looking haggard after some all-night debauch or stretched out in the Mediterranean sun, because the press go looking for him, not because he goes to more parties, night clubs and expensive holiday resorts than every other footballer or most young pop-music stars. But he is the antithesis of a self-publicist. He *wants* anonymity, but cannot possibly be permitted it: he is physically too arresting, too gifted, too retaliatory, too interesting. It is his own problem, and football's deep disappointment, that he is not equipped to absorb equably the attention he does not ask for, yet attracts so insistently.

It is tempting to set up Best as the defining representative of the modern British footballer – of the generation that has never known the constriction of a mandatory maximum wage and the modest lifestyle that went with it. But being the most glamorous, most talented and most brazenly rebellious of this generation does not make him characteristic of it. The point about Best that is of overriding importance is that he is unique. When he is considered as a footballer, ignoring his behaviour away from the pitch, one cannot find another player of any era to compare him with satisfactorily.

When he was introduced in Manchester United's First Division team, at 17, in September 1963 the immediate response of the writers and watchers of football was to welcome 'a second Stanley Matthews'. British football then was in love with, or at any rate gripped by, the new concept of the ever-running, passing and never-holding-the-ball player; the game was simultaneously busy and dull, and much more so than it is now, in spite of the current alarm at low scoring and declining attendances. So the slight figure of Best, as he dribbled the ball with endless invention around defenders, was a startling sight. There were charm and courage in this boy. (The degree of gratitude and affection that reporters and spectators felt for the shy, audacious young George has much to do, one feels, with the notable vindictiveness in the headlines and the spoken comment he is getting now.)

But it was not long before the parallel with Matthews, the shuffling dazzler of the thirties and forties, had to be abandoned. Best was seen to relish the thick of the in-fighting of a match in a way Matthews never did. Best liked to win the ball, possessing, as he still does, one of the most effective sliding tackles in the Football League. We saw Best to be aggressive as well as supremely subtle. He showed the kind of brave, almost reckless, improvisation that Matthews never attempted, taking the ball so close to a tackler that he could use the tackle itself against the defender. He would deliberately seek contact to claim the ball back off the opponent and thus dismiss him irrevocably.

In his most telling seasons with Manchester United, from 1964 to 1970, Best declared himself as a player almost without flaw: dribbling, passing, shooting, heading – all the skills were present in exceptional quality. Also there was a range in his game, the factor that is largely a matter of intuitive understanding of what ought to happen next – Danny Blanchflower had it, Pelé possessed it incomparably – and this was the extra dimension that made so massive an aggregate of the specific talents.

When Best was 18 he was already "a great player" in

the judgment of United's manager, Matt Busby, already a Northern Irish international. At 21 he was Footballer of the Year in England, the youngest ever. It is interesting to recall now that on the Saturday afternoon when he was told of this award he surprised us all with a little, acid impudence that momentarily opened up behind the shy, bland front. He was sitting, neat and gleaming from the bath, in Busby's huge office armchair, and he was dwarfed in it like a child. Someone asked him which player he would have voted for, and he said, with a twist of the lips, "Bobby Charlton's mother." (The story of Mrs Cissy Charlton's devoted 'coaching' of Bobby as a schoolboy player has long ago taken its place in the folklore of English football.) There was a gasp at the irreverence of the youth, before the room chuckled. Busby, who heard Best's reply as he was halfway out of the door, whipped round in embarrassment, only half smiling. "That's not for publication," he said. Best then bore the same wicked, mirthless grin that has come to be familiar as an accompaniment to his numerous, contemptuous dissensions with referees.

That incident has sprung to my mind frequently in the past five years. There was something in Best's manner, not arrogance or malice but a kind of disregard, a dismissiveness, an alone-ness, that affected the atmosphere. Here was a very young man, who didn't even look his age, who from the age of 15 had known only the insular, protected, self-nurturing world of the leading professional football club, who was so set apart as an individual that he could confuse its father-figure, normally so assured, and disconcert a score of men, most of them twice his age, by simply releasing a reflex action of the personality.

We, of course, established the atmosphere – the convention of a middle-aged, rather sentimental, very approving prize-giving. Best was neither intimidated nor much flattered, but his verbal flick of irritation was like the pound-for-pound kick on the ankle or jab of the elbow he was already beginning to deal out to tacklers in matches.

It is important to remember that Best reacts to the given situation. He is a singular man, a singular talent, in a team game, a collective approach, a group environment. If one can imagine his degree of individual ability projected into a man-for-man sport, like motor-racing or tennis, it's possible to see him in a very different light from the one we now are stuck with. Vivid, troublesome personality stands out much more sharply when it occurs in a component of a team. And it is Best's sad destiny that he appeared on the scene in English football when his club was already on the slide and its manager, that admirable and far-seeing man, was growing old and tired.

Manchester United have retained glamour by reputation and the astonishing longevity of Busby's reliance on forward play. But hindsight tells us what some of the players always knew: that the management and coaching and recruiting fell behind years ago in terms of firm grasp and energy and flair. Fortune helped to obscure the facts: United, with Busby as manager and Charlton as captain, won the European Cup in circumstances of unbearable emotion in 1968, with a weaker team and against weaker opposition than had contested the tournament in the three earlier years when Busby's team reached the semi-finals.

What kind of mature player might Best have become had he grown up with an improving team instead of a shakily established one? The question is imponderable. The man is father to the player; Best's skills come out of his personality, and the personality is informed by the rewards of its skills. Best is a conundrum: brilliance, uncertainty, wilfulness, vulnerability, callousness. He drinks too much; he regrets his drinking. He wants to find repose; he flits from girl to girl. He is capable of turning a game; he vaporises from it while you watch. He can be as charming as a child; he brushes his way through a crowd of children without a moment's pause.

If Best were a poet, or a ballet dancer, or an actor, his behaviour would both be less resented and less reported. But the British view of football is still very old-fashioned. Managers who were star players 20 or 30 years ago still insist, against the evidence of match after match, that the teams they played with were just as violent, just as committed. The hardcore of the game's following, which is of the managers' generation, likes to believe this.

Best was taken to its heart as long as he was a youth with youth's resilience – that blithe acceptance of outrageous ill-treatment from defenders. The grown man, who sees that his loyalty is to a poor side, who remembers the years when he was unprotected by inadequate referees, stubbornly supported by an ostrich-head of an executive, who knows he can only be slower in the future, and who shows his scars and turns in frustration and fear – I believe he is afraid of the future – to booze (sometimes), and fawning sycophants (regularly), offends this following because it cannot bear the accusation from the player that is implied.

Football expresses itself as much by the sound of its crowd as by the methods of its coaches. A separate man like Best is adored only as long as he rides the violence of the rest of the game. If he complains about it he is crying out of turn; if he joins it he is prostituting his God-given talent. Why wouldn't Best show some bewilderment?

He was born in Belfast, into a Protestant, working-class family, and that fact alone must be significant in considering his nature. In that environment, at its least an uneasy influence and commonly unbalancing, it is hardly surprising that a boy should acquire a *particular* attitude to authority, to the means of survival, to the pride of person. There was early enough evidence of his restlessness, his sensitivity to instruction.

United's scouting organisation picked him up when he was 15, and with another 15-year-old, the (now) Middlesbrough and Irish inside forward, Eric McMordie, he was delivered to the pebbledash council house in Chorlton-cum-Hardy where one of the club 'mums,' Mrs Mary Fullaway, had twin beds ready for them. Within 24 hours both were on a boat, going home. To this day Best insists that it was McMordie who was homesick; Mrs Fullaway smiles about that.

Best returned to Manchester, under Busby's persuasion, a fortnight later. But he had been an obstinate truant at school, and now he left the job the club found him as an office boy near the ground because he was not at ease with his employer. Did it matter? Of course not. Busby and his assistant, Jimmy Murphy, knew they had a player of rare gift. Best stood five feet three inches, and weighed four pounds under eight stone.

By the time he was 18 Best was famous. He was being paid between £70 and £100 a week (in 1964). At that stage he was still visibly and touchingly immature: tight suits, a sheen on his face, baby's brown eyes, a bag of sweets in his pocket, shyly playing snooker in a Temperance Hall. He was talking about the glamorous possibility of owning a sports shop when he was 21. There was a scrapbook on a table under the window of Mrs Fullaway's living room, and it had "George Best" written in painstaking, round characters on the cover. "A lovely lad," Mrs Fullaway said of him; and she has never said anything less.

When he was 21 how different it was: the gilded bachelor with a white Jaguar, photogenic girlfriends; the freedom of Manchester's night life, such as that awkward mimicry of Jermyn Street is; an agent, a secretary, boutiques with his name in gold paint; a blasé indifference to the needs and ambitions of the Ulster football team. Football had made him wealthy, given him a hard surface, begun to punish him physically.

The winter and spring of 1970 established Best the Problem Boy. In January he was fined £100 and suspended for a month, after knocking the ball out of the referee's hands in anger. In April he behaved so badly, when playing for Northern Ireland against Scotland in Belfast, that he soured the match irredeemably. After complaining to the referee, the Englishman, Eric Jennings, that a defender had dragged him away from the ball by his shirt, he picked up a handful of mud and threw it, with a mocking, girlish, under-arm gesture, at the official, and then spat at his feet. The crowd, overwhelmingly Irish, booed him as he was sent off.

Since then the list of misdemeanours, almost all of them more regrettable for their petulance and silliness than for any violence, has grown relentlessly. The more one thinks about his conduct the more saddened, rather than angered, one becomes. It's the money that gives so much pain. How recent were those marvellous, lilting soliloquies of his in the late sixties, yet how distant from his play now.

Alan Hardaker, the secretary of the Football League, told a national newspaper last week that he was tired of hearing Best's name. What a deep slough of dismal mean-mindedness is shown by our foremost football official with that wretched comment. Ten thousand Alan Hardakers don't make a minute of football. One hour of Best, at his most glorious, justifies the game: reminds us that it is capable of supreme theatre. If only we have a single George Best, as one remembers him resisting brutal tackles and whipping in a goal with that lift-less, electric action, we can even carry Alan Hardaker.

At the moment we do not have Best. It may be that English football will lose him to Spain, or Italy, or Holland. Even if he stays in England it is difficult to rid one's mind of the sense of obituary. Best is now 26. It is improbable that he can expect to rediscover the instant acceleration that made him so exciting – the loss is critical.

He has shown this season that if he really wants to do it, he can play in midfield to great effect. His club has yet to find another player, to replace Charlton, who can strike the ball with the accuracy and cunning that Best can achieve. He is as good a tackler, except for the young Scot, Buchan, as is available to the manager. There would be nothing demeaning, and much of value, in such a job for Best.

It seems, after last week's squalid sulking, that the rift is too wide for him ever to do it for Manchester United now. The question is whether Best can bring himself to work that way for anybody else. His nature resists anything so tedious as industry. Yet he would bring to it a beautiful intuition.

Observer Review, 19 December 1972

UNITED CALL IT A DAY
Eric Todd

Manchester United's most momentous day since the Munich disaster in February 1958 ended with the news that the club had dismissed Frank O'Farrell, its manager, Malcolm Musgrove, the chief coach, and John Aston, its chief scout. And if that were not enough for one day, George Best has made up his mind once and for all that he will never play football again.

The decisions were taken at a board meeting yesterday in the offices of United's chairman, Louis Edwards, and were released shortly after five o'clock. The statement read:

"In view of the poor position of the club in the

League, it was unanimously decided that Mr O'Farrell, Mr Musgrove, and Mr Aston be relieved of their duties forthwith. Furthermore, George Best will remain on the transfer list and will not be again selected for Manchester United as it is felt that it is in the best interests of the club that he leaves Old Trafford."

Mr O'Farrell had about three and a half years of his five-year contract still to run and this will be honoured, which means that he will receive about £40,000. The board stated further that Mr Musgrove and Mr Aston, who were not under contract, would receive "adequate compensation."

When Les Olive, United's secretary, arrived at Old Trafford to prepare for the afternoon's board meeting, he was handed a typed letter from George Best who, so far as was known, was unaware of the board's earlier decision.

It made interesting reading:

"I had thought seriously of coming personally and asking for a chance to speak at the board meeting, but once again I am afraid when it came to saying things face to face, I might not have been completely honest. I am afraid from my somewhat unorthodox ways of trying to sort my own problems out I have caused Manchester United even bigger problems.

"I wanted you to read this letter before the board meeting commenced so as to let you know my feelings before any decisions or statements are issued following the meeting.

"When I said last summer I was going to quit football, contrary to what many people said or thought, I seriously meant it because I had lost interest in the game for various reasons. While in Spain I received a lot of letters from both friends and well-wishers – quite a few asking me to reconsider. I did so and after weeks of thinking it over I decided to give it another try. It was an even harder decision to make than the original one.

"I came back hoping my appetite for the game would

return and even though in every game I gave 100 per cent there was something missing. Even now I am not quite sure what.

"Therefore I have decided not to play football again and this time no one will change my mind.

"I would like to wish the club the best of luck for the remainder of the season and for the future, because even though I personally have tarnished the club's name in recent times, to me and thousands of others Manchester United still means something special."

After the meeting, the directors made additional points. These included:

United have no replacement for Mr O'Farrell in mind, but he would not be a present member of the club, which rules out such possible candidates as Bobby Charlton and Bill Foulkes.

Best had broken his contract but the board had not discussed whether it would sue him. He still remained a registered player on United's books. The board had not been surprised by Best's letter.

Mr O'Farrell made a brief appearance before the board and took the news of his dismissal "quite well." He asked only two questions about his own contract and the position of Mr Musgrove. He was reassured on both counts.

Sir Matt Busby, asked if he thought his own presence at the club would be an embarrassment to potential applicants, replied: "I cannot understand this. I have always given full co-operation and since Frank O'Farrell came here he has had a completely free hand. We will have to try and get the lads to respond and do something for us until the appointment is made."

Guardian, 20 December 1972

BEST BACK WITH "NEW VALUES"
Eric Todd

A few days ago, a neighbour of mine and one of the older season-ticket holders at Old Trafford, rushed at me in the street and shouted: "Did you go last night? Absolute rubbish. The worst side United have had in years. Well, I've called him all the names under the sun and he has been a bloody fool, but I'd give a lot to see even half an hour of George Best." He may not have to wait long.

It appears that Best, footballer extraordinary, who in the past subscribed to no code of discipline unless he made it himself, and no code of loyalty unless it suited him, has decided that he would like once more to play football for Manchester United. But as far as I know, he is still on the transfer list, and so far as I remember, at least two United officials have said that he would never play for them again. And Best more than once has said that he had finished with football. Now United, warily perhaps, are considering giving Best another chance; maybe his third or is it fourth? No matter. Best, 10lb overweight, and "missing the game more than I thought possible," will report officially for training on Monday with a view, it may be assumed, to going back on the strength.

Best, who made his last appearance for United against Southampton on 25 November last year, returned from Spain last week, and shortly afterwards contacted Tommy Docherty. At a press conference in Manchester yesterday, Docherty said he was "delighted" to hear Best wanted to return. Best added: "I agreed to come back earlier, but got thrombosis in my leg, and this led to my going into hospital. Now the doctors say the leg is completely OK. Lying on my back for three weeks gave me plenty of time to think about things. Over the years I have caused some troubles, and I wasn't sure how they would receive me when I approached Mr Docherty this week."

It may well be that Docherty will have better luck with Best than did Sir Matt Busby and Frank O'Farrell, even though Best has not cultivated a Scottish accent, and may find some difficulty in re-adjusting himself. And mention of Docherty will pose the question: would he, or United, come to that, have been so ready to entertain a reformed Best if United had not made such a wretched start to the season? Is it more economical to take a gamble with Best than to spend £200,000 on somebody else?

Not even Best's sternest critics – and I am one of them – would deny that at the peak of his form, and before he became involved in the whirlpool of commerce and hectic living, Best was a genius. He may still be one. Whether he can get back to peak fitness after the spell in hospital where he says that he saw the light, and earn a place in the team, remains to be seen. If he can do both, United should be grateful and accept him back into the fold.

Speaking of his time outside the game, Best said: "I have always missed playing. It's the things outside football that create the pressures. This will have to be a comeback for keeps, otherwise everybody is just going to get sick of the situation.

"The longer I stayed away, the harder it was to come back. I have spoken to most of the other players recently, and they all told me they want me back. I would like to think that the drinking problems I had, and the depressions they caused, are behind me. These are things I have got to sort out myself, and prove to the public they are forgotten. I have got a new set of values. The only thing that has brought me back is that I have missed the game so much. In hospital I realised how much I was missing the game."

Nevertheless, Best faces a tremendous task, and it must be the final challenge to the better side of his character. He knows better than most that he let down the public no less than he let down United and himself.

He knows as well as anyone that many people hoped that they had heard the last of him. He knows better than anyone that he must mend his ways off the field as well as on it, where he has an ominous record of indiscipline.

Above all, he must spare no effort to show that he is sincere in his determination to win back his place in the team and in the estimation of the public. Frankly, I consider that he is a very lucky man indeed even to be allowed inside Old Trafford again, let alone given the chance of getting back into the side. If he justifies United's faith, then good luck to him; but as I have said before, I will believe it when I see it.

But if ever he transgresses again, please let there be no more attempts at salvage.

Guardian, 7 September 1973

GEORGE BEST CHARGED WITH THEFT
Gareth Parry

George Best was last night accused of stealing, among other things, Miss World's fur coat. Mr Best (27), described as a club owner, of Aycliffe Avenue, Chorlton, Manchester, was remanded on £6,000 bail at Marylebone Court.

He will appear there again on 27 March, charged with burglary and theft of property belonging to Miss Marjorie Wallace. His five minutes in court followed nearly five hours with the police at Paddington Green police station.

There he was formally charged with entering a building as a trespasser and stealing a fur coat, a passport, a cheque book, and other items belonging to the reigning Miss World, who lives in Park Square Mews, Marylebone, between 18 and 20 February. He was also charged with stealing spirits and correspondence worth £20, on 16 February.

His solicitor, Mr Geoffrey Miller, said before the court appearance that his client denied the charges.

Detective Chief Inspector Terence Finney said there was no objection to bail, but that he required an undertaking that Mr Best would not contact Miss Wallace. Mr Best said "Yes, sir" when asked if he agreed with this undertaking.

Bail consisted of a surety of £5,000 from his business partner, Mr Malcolm Wagner, of Hathaway Road, Bury, Lancashire, and £1,000 in his own recognisance.

Best became a star overnight when he joined Manchester United in 1963. He announced his retirement from football in 1972 while in the Spanish resort of Marbella, but six weeks later he changed his mind and started playing again.

In November he missed two training sessions, and went to London. On 5 December, he was put on United's transfer list, and two weeks later announced his retirement again.

Again he changed his mind, and returned to United in October 1973. Early last month, he failed to report for training, and has not returned to the club since. He remains on the team's transfer list.

His business interests include a Manchester night club, Slack Alice, and a travel agency.

News of his court appearance attracted crowds of sightseers and autograph hunters outside the building. Police diverted some of the crowd away from the rear entrance by using a decoy police car at the front door. Mr Best got away in the back of a police van.

Police halted traffic to give the van a clear escape route to where a fawn Daimler was waiting to take him home to Manchester.

COURT WILL DECIDE ON BEST CASE IN MONTH
Reporter

George Best was yesterday remanded on £2,000 bail until 24 April when, "come what may," the magistrate, Mr Kenneth Harington will either discharge him or commit him for trial by jury. Mr Best is charged with stealing a fur coat and other property belonging to the deposed Miss World, Marjorie Wallace.

Yesterday, however, the Marylebone magistrates' court was mainly concerned about the missing Miss Wallace, who is both the complainant and the prosecution's chief witness. She is in the US, having left Britain without notifying the police.

Mr Best had his bail reduced from £6,000 to £2,000. His solicitor, Mr Geoffrey Miller, argued that the original bail seemed "a disproportionate amount." Opposing this, Detective Chief Inspector Terence Feeney said that "people sometimes abscond."

Mr Miller asked: "Can you say that about Mr Best?"

Inspector Feeney: "I think it has been said of Mr Best in the past." However, he agreed it was unlikely that the former Manchester United star would disappear permanently.

A condition of bail was that Mr Best did not contact Miss Wallace directly or indirectly, which moved the magistrate to say: "Well, he would have a job to do that. We can't contact her ourselves."

The prosecutor, Mr Neil Denison, said that Miss Wallace was now in the State of Indiana. "The reason she is there at the moment is that she was a very close friend of the well-known American racing driver Peter Revson and that young man, unhappily, was killed last Friday in South Africa while practising for the Grand Prix." The burial would take place in Indiana tomorrow.

In these circumstances it was unreasonable to expect her to attend court although his information was that she "fully intends returning to this country for the proceedings provided a remand is granted this morning."

The magistrate said: "I take it you received a communication from the young lady that she would not be here?"

"Not from the young lady herself," Mr Denison replied.

Mr Miller, the defence solicitor, said that if the position was precisely as described by the prosecution, it would be unreasonable of him to oppose a further remand.

"I am instructed to say that Mr Best has nothing to fear if she attends," he added. But the facts were that Miss Wallace had left the country without telling the police several weeks ago, and it "just isn't true" that she was in America because of the death of Mr Revson.

"She says she doesn't intend to appear before the court," Mr Miller went on. "She has indicated to various sources that she doesn't intend to return to this case. Anyone who reads the papers knows that."

Mr Best had been humiliated, embarrassed, inconvenienced, and subjected to adverse publicity.

Guardian, 28 March 1974

BEST CLEARED BUT UNHAPPY AT PROCESS
Reporter

George Best was cleared yesterday of charges of stealing property from the flat of the former Miss World, Marjorie Wallace.

Mr David Miller, prosecuting, said at Marylebone, London, that Miss Wallace knew the date of the hearing "and she intimated that she does not want to attend." Accordingly the police could offer no evidence against Mr Best.

Mr Best, making his third court appearance on two charges, then formally pleaded not guilty and was told by the magistrate, Mr Kenneth Harington: "You are dismissed and I think I should add, as this matter has received a good deal of publicity, I should emphasise that you leave the court without a stain on your character."

Outside the court later Mr Best said: "I have been accused of some things in my time but never of being a petty thief. Of course I am glad the case is finally over but a dismissal of the charges is not the same as having the opportunity to prove my innocence in open court. But if that is the way it must be then I must accept it. Now I just want to forget all about it."

The first charge was that Mr Best had entered Miss Wallace's flat in Park Square Mews, Marylebone, between 18 and 20 February and stole a fur coat, a passport and other property. The second charge was that of stealing spirits and correspondence on 16 February.

On 27 March, at the prosecution's request, Mr Harington adjourned the hearing until yesterday because of Miss Wallace's failure to appear as a prosecution witness.

Yesterday Mr Miller said: "The position is that the police have been in touch with the police in America. It has not been possible to speak directly to Miss Wallace or to get in touch with her directly, but it is clear from information that the police have received in this country from the American police that Miss Wallace is aware of the court proceedings in this country.

"She is aware of the hearing and she has intimated that she does not propose to attend."

Mr Harington said: "Not a very keen witness in fact, really."

"No, sir," replied Mr Miller. He added that in this circumstance the position was plain. The prosecution did not have a case against Mr Best and therefore did not wish to proceed further.

A request by Mr Best's solicitor, Mr Geoffrey Miller, that the former football star should be allowed costs against the police was dismissed by Mr Harington.

Mr Miller's argument was that Mr Best was arrested "in the middle of the night" and "police were notified by me at 6.30 a.m. that he had a complete answer to the charge and that he had an absolute alibi."

The defence had always contended that "these charges were misconceived and should not have been brought in the first place. It appears to the defence, having regard to what we have been told and what evidence has been made available to us, that this prosecution was based on the uncorroborated evidence of this young lady who had not attended." Mr Best had been subjected to a "very unfortunate and unnecessary experience."

But Mr Harington said costs were only allowable if the defence could show that the charge was not brought in good faith.

Mr Miller replied that as no evidence had been heard, it was clearly impossible for him to show that.

Mr Best had been accompanied to court by Mr Michael Parkinson, the writer and television personality. He was driven in a chauffeured Rolls-Royce. After the hearing he ran to a Mercedes but this car only took him round a corner where he re-entered his Rolls-Royce and was then driven away.

In court no mention was made of the fact that some of the articles taken from Miss Wallace's flat were returned anonymously, during the period of Mr Best's remand, to the *Sunday People* newspaper together with notes declaring that Mr Best was innocent.

Guardian, 25 April 1974

DUNSTABLE DREAMING OF YOUNG BROWN EYES
Julie Welch

If you can unclog your memory as far back as last February, when football seemed to have been granted an unconditional divorce from George Best, you may have been delighted or apoplectic, depending upon your feelings for the young man, to hear that eight days from now the nuptials are scheduled again. The reception will take place at Dunstable, the honeymoon will last for an as-yet undefined period, and the role of cupid has been shared by Barry Fry (manager) and Keith Cheeseman (chairman) of Dunstable Town FC.

It won't be much like the first time round, of course. The famous rolltop-desk eyelids may still bat heart-rendingly, and the mane may be as luxuriantly kempt as ever, but gone are the days when Best was worth more pounds sterling per toenail than the massed plates of meat of an average First Division side.

Dunstable isn't exactly one of the heavily-shaded portions of the footballing map. Not that it's any the worse for that. A quiet, respectable place within shouting distance of Luton. No yowling transistors destroying the calm, no nasty supporters breaking up the amenities in the High Street of a dull winter Saturday. At the ground – and the club officials would be the first to admit that there are in existence football grounds of a more *soigné* nature – the noise of the crowd might often in the past have been drowned by the cacophony of bird life in the woodland behind the far goal.

Last season the club attracted gates of around 100 – but that is hardly surprising, since Dunstable Town finished bottom of the Southern League's First Division North.

It wasn't really their fault. Until the advent last February of Mr Cheeseman, the club operated on a budget that was less like a shoestring than a pair of broken laces, and remained in existence mainly through the zeal and enthusiasm of men like its secretary, Harold Stew. Up and down the country there are, of course, many small clubs similarly burdened, but they don't have a Mr Cheeseman with a cheque book and pen poised at the ready.

Well, not yet, anyway. For, it seems, Mr Cheeseman intends to take over three struggling Southern League clubs, install greyhound tracks and run them as a commercial venture. Last week he put £10,000 into Bedford Town and became a majority shareholder, and he is now making wooing noises towards Stevenage Athletic.

Whether this attempt at coffer-swelling will be a success remains to be seen, but his appearance as Mr Bountiful has been extremely good for Dunstable. And while no one could accuse him of doing it all out of sheer altruism, it was not so many years ago that Keith Cheeseman, stripling, turned out for Dunstable Town reserves.

Cheeseman the footballer may not have illuminated Beds., Bucks. and Herts. with his mazy dribbles or salmon-leap headers, but Cheeseman the builder has, at 32, done very nicely for himself as managing director of a large West Midlands company, and if you can't beat 'em, buy 'em, that's what they always say.

He has already bought Jeff Astle, late of West Bromwich Albion, England, and that famous gaping goalmouth in Mexico. He fancied the look of Sir Alf Ramsey as adviser, and would have bought him except that Sir Alf wasn't havin' none of that. He was also lucky that Fry, Dunstable's manager, had been in the Manchester United youth team with Best and had kept contact with him despite the widely divergent paths their respective careers took.

Of course, Dunstable do not yet possess Best forelock, stock and barrel. So far, they've got Manchester United's permission to play him in only two friendlies before the start of the season. The first one will take place on 5 August, probably against West Bromwich Albion. Between now and then the club staff will be getting ready with their paint pots and their cleaning fluid, because right now Creasey Park is no showcase to put their museum-pieces in.

For a start, "stands" is rather a euphemism for the seating accommodation. "Prones" would be a better term at present, since three weeks ago part of the main stand burned down and, some time before that, the east stand, after a gale, adopted the posture of an elderly lady drunk. It is without question, however, that the splendid Mr Stew, who has been with Dunstable Town since 1950, will, by some miracle of minor engineering and whitewash, have got things ready for the expected influx of 5,000 people.

Five thousand, because, as Mr Fry says, "How can you put in words what it means getting George Best at Dunstable? It'll be a bigger boost for the club than having Frank Sinatra sing at half time."

I don't like to start a rumour but, if Young Brown Eyes is back, how much longer can it be before Ol' Blue Eyes, too, succumbs to the advances of K. Cheeseman?

Observer, 28 July 1974

FLOATING OFF ON A RED AND WHITE BALLOON

JOHN ARLOTT reviews Michael Parkinson's book on the life and times of George Best

By the normal standards of sports book publishing, one can hardly imagine anything more untimely than a life of George Best in 1975. Michael Parkinson's *Best* (Hutchinson), though, does not conform to the normal standards of sports book publishing. Indeed, it is in direct contrast to the weary, ghosted "autobiography" that reduced the genre to the lowest literary level in the hardback trade.

This is not simply a sports book; it is a valid piece of creative writing irrespective of its classification. The "timely" book on the subject, with the title – slick then, ironic now – *Best of All Worlds* was published in 1968: it spoke for a successful footballer with an international "pop" image.

This is a study of the man who serves drinks in a Manchester night club called Slack Alice's; one who had completed a career at 28. That was virtually Michael Parkinson's only asset when he wrote *Best* – his story had a clear beginning and end. The measure of his success is not only that he enabled Best's admirers to understand him – and themselves – better; but that it will lead many who regard him with contempt to understanding. He has sub-titled it "an intimate autobiography" and each chapter ends with a section of "George's Story," in effect the subject's psychologist's couch view of the situation. Like the life it illuminates, it is full of four-letter words: it would be false if it were not. There are more girls than goals, but the goals are serious. "I remember every game I ever played in, good and bad. I've got my own action replay. I can run it through my mind at will."

Those who dismiss George Best because of his long hair, beard and behaviour ignore his importance. If sport is important, George Best is important; if sport is historic, this book is history. "Busby's ambition was to win the European Cup. The dream he nurtured privately was that one day he might find another player to match Duncan Edwards. The ambition he knew to be possible, the dream he believed was hopeless but harmless.

"In February 1961 he took a 15-year-old Belfast boy on to his playing staff, and, although he didn't know it at the time, by doing so he achieved his ambition and fulfilled his dream. The boy's name was George Best and, from the moment he signed for United, nothing was the same again, not for Sir Matt, nor for the club, and most certainly not for George Best."

Michael Parkinson is not content with his own opinion of Best's footballing ability. Danny Blanch-flower – comparing him with Matthews and Finney – "George Best gets my vote. A master of control and manipulation, he is also a superb combination of creator and finisher, he can play anywhere along the line. More than the others he seems to have a wider, more appreciative eye for any situation; the more refined, unexpected range; and an utter disregard of physical danger."

That sharply observant Scottish footballing crafts-man Paddy Crerand thought "He could do more things better than any player I have ever seen." Sir Matt Busby – "George Best was gifted with more individual ability than I have ever seen in any other player, certainly unique in the number of gifts." These are the rare and measured superlatives of authority; and they place Best on a plane where many of his characteristics are irrelevant.

Best himself recalls the crucial semi-final leg of the 1968 European Cup, against Real Madrid – when Manchester United were losing 3-1 at half time. "In comes the boss (Matt Busby). We think we're going to get a right bollocking and we deserved it because we were awful. But he just looks in and says 'Right lads, go out there and keep playing football.' And I started bloody laughing. I mean, there's this old bugger who'd give his left arm to win the sodding cup and we're screwing it up for him and he tells us to keep on playing football. I thought that was a bit special." In the second half Best made the goal that won the tie; and he settled the final by scoring himself.

Michael Parkinson looks at him then – "He had just completed a season when he added new dimensions to his already staggering range of gifts. He had merged two life-styles, soccer and show biz into one. He was an athlete and an entertainer, a soccer player and a sex symbol, an adolescent and a working class hero. By middle class standards he was well off, about £150 a week, two boutiques in Manchester and a fish and chip shop in Belfast which he bought his parents. He was voted footballer of the year, polling 60 per cent of the votes and the only question was, who on earth did the other 40 per cent vote for?"

Again and again he produces the significant. Sir Matt Busby is talking to Best: "We'll look after you, and all you have to do is keep fit, live like an athlete and you can retire when you are thirty if you want. Now, does that seem too difficult?" "Yes," said George.

Best was value for the media – "I liked that journalist. Every time she wanted a story she used to come and stay with me in Manchester. That's what I call good press relations." The press were not present – but his biographer was – when he said – "A lot of people in my position end up topping themselves, but that will never happen to me. I'd be so frightened of missing something. I keep remembering a scene from the film *Charlie Bubbles*. I think that is how I'd like it to end. Just floating away in a bloody great big balloon with red and white stripes on it."

With infinite perception and unobtrusive skill Michael Parkinson has created a study of a remarkable footballer and unaccountable person. It is not his fault that it is a spiritual obituary. He leaves all the last words with Best.

In the final paragraph he is watching a World Cup match on television. At a crucial juncture a player "scores" with a penalty, but is ordered to retake it. As he puts the ball on the spot the commentator says "Who would want to be in his shoes at this moment?" "Oh, I would," said George Best. "Oh, I bloody would."

Guardian, 13 March 1975

BEST RETURNS WITH A GOAL FOR STOCKPORT
Paul Fitzpatrick

George Best, one of the finest footballers Britain has ever produced, but sadly one of the game's most unpredictable personalities, took his first tentative steps on the way to a resumed football career at Edgeley Park last night when he played for Stockport County in a fund-raising game with Stoke City, a club desperately keen to sign him.

Best, given a free transfer by his old club Manchester United, last Saturday, has joined Stockport for a month and may play for them in a League match against Swansea City on 28 November. Before last night's match, however, Tony Waddington, the Stoke manager, reiterated his determination to sign Best.

In the meantime Best will attempt to recover his old fitness. He has adopted a level-headed approach to the chance of a renewed career. He is a long way from the fitness and sharpness that the First Division would demand but Best is well aware of that. He fully accepts that much hard work lies ahead if he is to return to the game, and he says he will not make a return unless he can do himself justice.

Not surprisingly Best last night adopted a policy of non-involvement. For the most part he spent his time on the left wing, a Puskas-like figure scarcely exerting himself but occasionally producing magical moments – a fierce drive from 30 yards that dipped just wide of a post, an exquisite pass, a bewildering change of direction. Once he reacted tenaciously to losing the ball by immediately winning it back. He shook the crossbar with a left-foot shot and, to the unbounded delight of numerous boys, he scored a fine goal from a free kick. And Best had paced himself so well that his involvement in the second half was much more committed.

Because of his wayward past it is impossible to anticipate how Best's future will develop. Waddington, nevertheless, insists that he would not be taking a gamble signing the player even though it is 20 months since Best last played League football. Certainly there can be no denying his magnetism. Last night a crowd of 8,081 went to Edgeley Park, almost four times the normal attendance and one of Stockport's biggest crowds for years. Although Stoke to their credit turned out a strong side, including Hudson, there was no doubt whom most people had come to watch.

The match itself, apart from Best's appearance and the fact that it must have given a welcome boost to Stockport's needy coffers, was of little significance. For the record Moores gave Stoke the lead in the 59th minute and Best equalised almost immediately.

Guardian, 11 November 1975

BEST BACK IN STYLE
Alan Dunn

Stockport County: 3
Swansea City: 2

George Best chose workaday Edgeley Park for his return to League football and Stockport County were highly grateful, for without him they would have found Swansea City too well drilled and progressive.

Best paced himself sensibly, as becomes a man not yet fully fit, but his lissom dribbling and perceptive passing still created the kind of electricity that was last seen at Edgeley Park when the elegant Alex Young moved there from Everton seven years ago.

Best announced himself with a delicious flicked pass after four minutes, felt his way carefully through an assortment of tackles, created County's first two goals, and crowned it all with a beauty of a goal. It was all highly flattering for County, who were made to struggle throughout the first half by the insistence and fitness of Leach, Curtis, and James, with Smith delighting in coming forward. But all of them missed perfect opportunities and Swansea had nothing to fall back on when Best struck.

The first goal after 20 minutes was the product of three consecutive corners from the left by Best, the first two tauntingly close to the near post and the third flighted perfectly slightly farther for Potter to turn the ball into his own net. In the 55th minute Best burst down the left, jinked past three men, and centred for Bradley to score firmly. Then, 17 minutes later, Best sent Seddon away on the right. Bradley headed back Seddon's centre, and Best was there to volley home with his left foot.

Stockport County: Hopkinson; Turner, Buckley, Lawther, Bradley, Fogarty, Best, Seddon, Hollis, Massey, McNeil.
Swansea City: Potter; W. Evans, Davies, Smith, P. Evans, Harris, Lalls, Curtis, James, Gray, Leach.
Referee: J. Sewell (Quorn).

Guardian, 29 November 1975

BEST TAKES THE CURE
Hugh McIlvanney

The calendar lay trampled in a corner for a while in the visitors' dressing-room at Old Trafford on Wednesday evening. Even when the door was open the place was hermetically sealed within its own atmosphere, a time-capsule with the smell of embrocation.

Outside in the corridor, and out on the field beyond when the action was under way, it was inescapably 1975 and whatever was competitive about the occasion belonged to the young and the vigorous, to those whose ambition in football is still raw and urgent and unabated by achievement. But inside that room, trapped in the bantering camaraderie of an unlikely reunion, was the feeling of the sixties, of those seasons when Law, Best, Charlton, Crerand, Stiles and the rest gave Manchester United a surging excitement and effectiveness that made them the most admired team in the Football League and the only one of its members to take the European Cup.

They had reassembled to play in a testimonial match for Pat Crerand but there was nothing perfunctory about their coming together. All of them knew this was something remarkable.

It was, apart from anything else, almost certainly the last time Denis Law will be seen kicking a ball in earnest before the public and the last time his relentlessly mischievous tongue will be heard in a dressing-room. It was also another intriguing opportunity to gauge the realities of George Best's attempt to reclaim some of the years of a great career that he buried under a rubble of irresponsibility and seeming indifference to his high talent.

To a privileged interloper under the stands at Old Trafford the juxtaposition of Law and Best at this point of their lives was fascinating and not a little poignant. In general, give or take a few disappointments, Law fulfilled himself in football. He left the game soon after his powers began to fade and long before there was a danger of being an embarrassment to the memory of his best days.

Now he works in the carpet business in Blackburn, learning all he can about it and applying himself to its nine-to-five demands with an eagerness that surprises only those who do not know him well.

Conscientiousness is basic to him. He trained specially for Wednesday evening's match – running round the darkened streets near his home with two of his four sons – and then slept fitfully through Tuesday night because of worry about how he would perform. "You have standards and you don't want to fall too far below them," he said after showing sufficient glimpses of his old electric menace to justify the flood of acclaim that would have come in any case from a crowd who will always call him The King. "I didn't do so bad tonight and that was a relief, but I'll never put myself through the ordeal again. No way. To play football properly you must train every day. Otherwise, forget it."

For a long time Best, having found that training every day was more than his social schedule could stand, did try to forget football but now, five months short of his 30th birthday, he is struggling with the pains of a resurrection that will hardly be remembered for its stealth. A health farm has given expensive help with the shedding of weight and a string of matches of varying seriousness has provided encouraging evidence that the touch skills, the tight control with both feet, the deadliness of shot, the mental alertness and aggressive imagination have all suffered minimal erosion from inactivity. Sadly and inevitably missing from that list is the explosive acceleration that was always central to his greatness.

Yet without it he still has far more equipment than most top professionals today, enough to add thousands to any League club's gate and certainly enough to swell the stream of financial inducements that is coming his way. As we talked in the dressing-room, a man intervened to slap a piece of paper in Best's hand and mutter about "a match in Delhi and a match in Calcutta." When Best inquired if the proposals contained any specific mention of "readies" the emissary was non-committal. "Calcutta?" Best said when he had gone. "Just my scene." Not entirely, but nothing is out of the question if the money is right. As he thrust his soiled boots into his bag afterwards, he laughed and said, "I wonder where the hell these'll come out next. They've been all over England this month."

They were doing damage again at Stockport on Friday, of course, but that was just another staging post on a long uphill road that must reach a fork soon, with one route leading towards the United States and the other towards one of several British clubs who are willing to bet on his talents and his drawing power, perhaps to the extent of paying him up to £1,000 an appearance.

"At the moment it looks like the States," he said. "When I've turned out in the couple of games I'm playing for Stockport and brought my fitness along a bit more, I think I'd like to go over there for the four months of their season. Then when I saw how far that had taken me towards what I was, I could make up my mind on more of a long-term basis. I don't know how much of my pace I'll get back, but I'm sure I'll get a lot more than I have now. So far I've been concentrating on general conditioning, doing no work on explosive sprints."

Sitting on the bench seat with a towel across his lap, his body – under the dark hair which is so thick on his chest that it almost looks like an extension of his beard – betrayed residual softness in the torso and what may be permanent thickening of the legs. The body will harden if he continues to force his weight closer to 11 stone but all of us who wish him well would have more faith in the fairy-tale if medical science had perfected the will transplant and Denis Law were available as a donor.

Best can show all the determination in the world in short bursts – as in a football match – but it is the other, slow-burning kind he needs now and he has never stood still long enough to be measured for a monk's habit. The persistent stories that he is short of money could suggest a new and pressing incentive but he denies them directly, though with no eruption of indignation.

"Coming back was a lot more appealing when

Manchester United gave me a free transfer. While I was still on their books there was always a terrible rigmarole of clearing it with them if I wanted to play anywhere. Now that's out of the way and obviously if I put myself in shape there's real money about but I'm really attracted at the thought of playing well again. I've come to miss the game badly and I miss it more because I know in my heart I could still be at the top."

Whatever ache there is would be intensified on Wednesday as he sat quietly under the peg with his clothes on it and listened to the distant rumble of the crowd and the boisterous chat of Law. Taking a moment off from playfully lacerating his friends, Law answered my question about how his boys were shaping as footballers: "I've told them they're not touching a ball until they're 15. Until then they're only allowed to kick people. That way they should become real modern professionals."

Later, more seriously, he said: "You know, I miss the dressing-room more than the park. As your body slows, you become resigned to the fact that you have to stop playing. Playing is a great experience, magic, irreplaceable, but you know it's got to end. Somehow you think the kind of comradeship you have in the dressing-room, the emotion and the excitement and all the laughs you have there, should go on. Then you realise that, too, has gone for ever. It's hard to take."

George Best may yet stave off the blow for a year or two. I'm not confident, just sincerely hopeful.

Observer, 30 November 1975

A TUBBY TOUCH OF PUSKAS
Frank Keating

It was quite like old times at Craven Cottage. "Show us how, Georgie," said a bedroom banner in Kenyon Road. "Welcome home Rodney," said one in Inglethorpe Street. A rattling good crowd in high good humour, Tommy Trinder offloading his very worst jokes (always a good sign) and Rodney Marsh back where he belongs. But it was George Best that everybody came to see. And he played a fine, mature game too. By the way, Bristol Rovers were the opposition.

Over 21,000 people paid a record £19,000 to see it. Fulham averaged 10,000 lost souls last season in a ground that holds 40,000. Dads took their sons and daughters, their sisters and their cousins and their aunts. Also, there were hundreds of middle-aged once dynamic baldies who had crawled out of the corduroy fifties to relive their youth.

Best scored with a swerving, bobbling shot after only 70 seconds. It was the only goal. Best had last come to the Cottage in the mid-sixties when Manchester United carved up the Lilywhites. A lot of vodka-and-lemonade has passed under the bridge, and, on Best's own admission, more girls than goals. But he has changed, he says, he really has. Fulham, he insists, will not regret their confidence in him.

Certainly, in the middle for an hour-and-a-half he repaid their daring most handsomely. Well, for an hour anyway. He ran out of puff at the end. He is not slim, but at least he is slimmer than his Slack Alice days. There is a tubby touch of Puskas about him now. But his first-half performance was, in the circumstances of considerable pressure, a splendid one. He lurked around the middle reaches, slinging out long balls to either wing as though he was Bobby Charlton incarnate – or, dare one say it, Johnny Haynes.

It was a treat to watch him work with Marsh. That

worthy perspired far more than usual to save himself being upstaged. They each responded gloriously to each other, both holding orthodoxy to be a servant not a master. All their schemes were born from an unconscionable adventure. Whether you like it or not Best is heir to Matthews, or even Finney; Marsh is heir to Shackleton. With reasonable luck it will be well worth a long trip wherever Fulham are playing.

Best's decisive goal should have been stopped by Eadie – but that grunting, red-jerseyed goalkeeper knew a good story when he saw one, as did we all. But Eadie spiked George's punchline at the very end when, after a rippling run across the face of some devilish angry tackles, our new hero had his corking 20 yard shot gloriously fingered away.

Afterwards George said he was going to have a quiet evening at home in Buckinghamshire with his photogenic, double-barrelled blonde – "it's really steady this one, I've known her over three months" – to eat early and watch the Parkinson Show. I wonder if he did? Certainly the hope is that this Huckleberry Finn might just have found his Mississippi down by the friendly Thames.

As Rodney said afterwards: "Listen mate, if only 50 per cent of what we two try together comes off, it will still be 200 per cent more than any other wanker in the League." And this morning, anyway, Fulham deserve applause for giving that sort of theory a go.

Guardian, 6 September 1976

SUNSHINE AND BEST
Frank Keating

George Best exhibited another riveting little cameo for Fulham on Saturday, yet to the pedantic mandarins of

Lytham St Anne's he is still on trial. Not until his probationary three-month period is up in two weeks' time, say these astonishing bureaucrats, will they give their decision on whether the Irish wizard will be allowed to stay and earn his crust in League football.

Just what can they be up to, when here we all are grasping and begging for the veriest crumb of quality? Even now, George Best remains one of the very, very few players with the ability to let the sunshine blaze through the dowdy, grey skies of our national professional game. Indeed, there is a case for the Lancashire pin-stripes to flop onto their knees and plead with George to stay among us. We need him more than he needs us, this Huckleberry who really seems to have found his Mississippi down at the lazy, lovely old Thames.

On Saturday against Oldham – just as he had done the week before at Blackpool, apparently – Best not only chased and harried with single-minded fervour on a skid-pan pitch, but warmed the very cockles with a collection of outrageously silky doodles that all the swank art galleries should have been falling over themselves to buy. He had some sort of hand in all Fulham's five goals, and in scoring the fourth himself, he put his signature to a glorious day with an exquisite flourish.

Twenty yards from goal, and dead in front, he fastened on to a loose ball; no one to pass to, two pals ahead of him were offside. He lazily beat a man, sensed the goalkeeper straying from his line, so he chipped the thing over his head in the gentlest parabola, like Nicklaus caressing his way out of the wickedest sand trap. The ball kissed the crossbar on the way, fell over the line and dropped dead, with the poor goalie on his backside and all of us beside ourselves with the marvel of it.

If that was the virtuoso's solo, the goal before it was, collectively, almost as thrilling. This time Best, deep inside his own half, sold some slithering hatchetman a dummy de-luxe, released Mitchell with a stunning 40-yard pass and Maybank's forehead thundered home the centre. Maybank had already scored the second and Mitchell got the first and last. They both played very well, strapping enthusiasts each. Who will make room for Marsh when that worthy's pirouetting ankle mends? Neither of them on this form.

In fact, Maybank is only on a month's loan from Chelsea. This was his first home match. The crowd loved his galumphing (sic) charges. If he settles, Fulham had thought to buy him for about £30,000. Chelsea could well ask for double after this little lot. Maybank's month finishes on Christmas Eve, so if a deal falls through he could yet be playing against Fulham in West London's Boxing Day derby. Dear old Fulham, they remain surely the most perplexing team of all to support. When Marsh and Best arrived the home crowd swelled to 21,000 for the first four home games. Three bad defeats halved that. Meanwhile, though, away grounds have been packed to see the show. A few more days like Saturday and Craven Cottage will be bursting again, I warrant.

Oldham, by the way, contributed a sturdy fairness to the afternoon. If their promotion ambitions are to be considered seriously, though, they really must start getting some visiting form together. Not that anyone could do much about Fulham and Best on Saturday, mind you.

Guardian, 6 December 1976

BEST IN A SPIDER'S WEB
Richard Yallop

The FA yesterday charged George Best with bringing the game into disrepute by his gesture of an explicit sexual nature to John Homewood, the referee, at the end of Fulham's League match with Chelsea at Stamford Bridge on 7 December. Fulham now have seven days in which to decide whether to ask for a personal hearing for Best or to send their version of the incident in a report to the FA.

The incident came at the end of a fiercely contested match in which Best was largely unprotected against the excesses of Chelsea's tackling. Lacy and Evanson of Fulham had both been booked by Homewood for foul play before Best was tackled recklessly from behind by Droy, a foul ignored by the referee.

Best made his gesture to Homewood as he left the field. Best was sent off in Fulham's game against Southampton in October.

It was for a verbal insult of a similar nature that it had been assumed that whatever disciplinary points were awarded against Best for the booking at Stamford Bridge would be added to his existing total of 16 points, leading to his possible suspension. But as Best was booked after the final whistle had blown, the FA have now brought this separate charge against him, which will not affect his points tally. An FA official yesterday confirmed that the decision to charge Best was taken as a result of the referee's report, and he was not in fact cautioned.

Best is due to discuss the case with Fulham's manager, Bobby Campbell, and other club officials today, when they will consider the disparaging remarks that Homewood was reported to have made to the Fulham players after they had protested to him about Droy's tackle on Best.

Homewood himself yesterday refused either to confirm or deny that he had made these remarks to some of the Fulham team. Best said that he considered the referee's words did more to bring the game into disrepute than his action.

Guardian, 5 January 1977

BE EXPLICIT ABOUT BEST
Frank Keating

A selection of readers' letters

The Football Association's disciplinary action against George Best following his barney with the referee after Fulham's match with Chelsea has inspired our writing readers. For a start, Donald Campbell, of Hull, wants to know what the player actually *did* to bring the game into disrepute, an act which most correspondents described coyly as "a gesture of explicitly sexual nature."

He writes: "I presume it was the same as that which got Harvey Smith into trouble. Since that incident I have asked a fair number of people to interpret the exact meaning of the V-sign. They all know the general drift of the message, but none has been sure what it represents in detail or why it has to take the very precise form to be understood. Does the FA know? Anyway, surely, Fulham's best riposte would be to ask the FA what is explicit about the sexual nature of the gesture."

Actually, Best wasn't guilty of Harvey's V-sign. As they were leaving the field, the Irishman is alleged to have called the referee, John Homewood, "Mr Wanker" – and accompanied the proper noun with an "improper", limp-wristed gesture. Donald Paterson, of East Grinstead, saw the match and thought Mr Homewood's performance with the whistle very poor (so did I, as it happens). He writes:

"I am not saying that Mr Homewood – or referees in general – should be crucified on the strength of this particular match but it is certainly asking too much of a little man in black to be asked to play God in a kingdom of 22 grown (and very human) men, whose very livelihood and reputation depend on his judgments. I cannot believe that Solomon, with all his wisdom, would have volunteered for the job.

"Can we not take lessons from other games which have either, like hockey, started off with a more practical system of control or have adjusted themselves to the current scene by the use of sophisticated electronic devices. Why should football chance the criticism of a goal allowed in extra time, when a remote stop watch and a hooter could define the matter precisely?

"I hold no special brief for George Best, but I am sure that he and many others are largely the victims of circumstances created by the outmoded attitude of the Football Association. Without wishing to widen the argument too far, may I say that it is, perhaps, more than coincidental that the state of English soccer is at its lowest ebb at this time."

Guardian, 26 December 1977

BEST IS FINED
Richard Yallop

George Best was yesterday fined £75 by an FA Disciplinary Commission after being found guilty of bringing the game into disrepute. The charge arose from the gesture Best made to John Homewood, the referee, at the end of Fulham's Second Division match at Stamford Bridge on 27 December. Best was ordered also to pay the costs of yesterday's hearing and warned about his future conduct.

The fine is in line with the FA's most recent punishments. On 11 January Andy Gray of Aston Villa was fined £75 for making a V-sign to a section of the Villa crowd during the home match against Manchester United and Alan Mullery was fined £100 for making the same gesture to Crystal Palace supporters and haranguing the referee, Ron Challis, after Brighton had lost their FA Cup replay with Palace at Stamford Bridge.

The comparative leniency of Best's punishment helps discount the player's own fears that he has been victimised by the authorities since his return from America. Best's one comment as he left the hearing was that he was satisfied he had received a fair hearing, a sentiment echoed by his manager, Bobby Campbell, who said: "It was well worth dashing back from the Channel Islands and the work involved in getting all the evidence together." Fulham played a friendly in Guernsey at the weekend.

The three-man commission sat for 90 minutes before giving their verdict. They called on Ted Drake, Fulham's chief scout, to give evidence, but Fulham's other two witnesses, Bobby Moore, and Colin Mapham, a radio reporter with London Broadcasting, were not summoned.

Fulham submitted a transcript of Mapham's comments on the match, which criticised Homewood's handling, to the commission. During the game Best was subjected to some rough Chelsea tackling and a particularly heavy challenge by Droy, immediately before the end, provoked Best's response. A number of Fulham's players complained to Mr Homewood that Droy had not been cautioned for the tackle.

Another part of Fulham's defence was to have centred on insults Homewood is alleged to have made to Best and other members of the Fulham team as they left the field. Bobby Moore was one of the players who heard the remarks being made. Best has said Homewood's remarks did more to bring the game into disrepute than his own gesture, and the number of matches Homewood is given between now and the end of the season is likely to provide the final comment on the affair.

Guardian, 1 February 1977

HOW I HIT THE POST, BY BEST
Reporter

The soccer star George Best yesterday described the car accident which has put him out of football for six weeks.

In his room at St Stephen's Hospital, South West London, he said: "I pulled in to go inside another car and clipped the kerb. As I hit the kerb I lost a wheel and went up the pavement and collided with a lamp post. Now I can't do anything for a month at least."

Propped up in bed, sipping orange juice, Best said: "My face is not too bad, but my shoulder is the thing that hurts more than anything."

Best, who is 30, has cuts, bruises and a minor fracture of his shoulder after his crash near Harrods in Brompton Road, Knightsbridge, early on Thursday.

Asked if he would be returning to California to convalesce, he said: "I should think Fulham will want me to stay here. It's just a question of getting this right first, then I'll be back playing."

He described his evening before the crash. "I had been out to dinner and called in at Tramp (the West End night club) to arrange for somebody to get in as my guest the next night. I wasn't given a breath test after the accident; and even if I had been it would have been negative. I had three drinks all evening."

Doctors believe that the cuts on Best's forehead – some of them stitched – will heal and not spoil his looks. Best said that he had only been involved in one serious accident before. "I collided with a pedestrian, but when I phoned the hospital to see if he was OK they said he had disappeared," he said. "Apart from that, I've only had the normal bumps and scrapes."

One visitor at the hospital yesterday was Best's former fiancée, Angela McDonald-James.

Guardian, 26 February 1977

GEORGIE PORGIE RAN AWAY . . .
Frank Keating

I fancy he really means it this time – and we won't be seeing George Best performing again for real on a British football field. At least he might have waited two more days before flying away to a place that, agreed, probably understands him better. For at least, I am sure, some of us then would have packed trains to have given him a decent curtain call this afternoon at Tottenham's White Hart Lane.

As it was, his cheerio seems to have been last Saturday at Craven Cottage in front of just a handful when Fulham played a tired and tawdry Second Division goalless draw with Blackburn Rovers. Like the man said: "Much Ado About Nothing–Nothing." I know, because I was there.

As hack of all trades, I was due to cover the London to Brighton walk. The boss rang first thing on Saturday. Don't walk, run up to Essex on Sunday for the cricket. Hooray. A Saturday off! What shall we do, darling? Shopping? Visiting? A trip to the country? Busmen understand: Georgie was back – so of course we went to Craven Cottage.

Best said he had arrived from Los Angeles only the teatime before, he had checked his English bank statement and found that Fulham (whose financial palavers had kept the newspapers' summer silly season going) had not paid what he reckoned they had promised him, but he had turned out last Saturday "in good faith and to keep my side of the bargain." Jet-lagged and tan-legged he had played a wizard game in the circumstances. Even at 31 he was a thought ahead of the 21-year-olds.

Not realising it so relevant as it has become, I must applaud that my mind played flashbacks in the drowsing sun last Saturday: I thought of his steamship arrival at Manchester 16 long years ago, when he had taken a taxi from Piccadilly Station and been dumped and frightened at the Old Trafford cricket ground and left on the next day's ship to go back to mum.

Then his first game for United against West Brom 14 years ago this autumn when David Meek, of the *Manchester Evening News* said his "exciting natural talent will brighten even the dullest of games . . ." Then when he scored one or two, and laid on a couple of others right through the super sixties, or even when he scored six or seven himself in the Cup against Northampton and, without any arrogance, said at the end that the goalie had played well . . . Or in 1968 when he first stormed Spain single-handed to take his senior men to a final against Portugal, and then, in extra time, to hand Sir Matt the European Cup . . . Or when he dummied Gordon Banks of England to make him look a jerseyed fool . . . And a thousand wonderful weekends right down to wintry Fulham Saturdays last year.

By then he was out to grass and we had thought this Huckleberry had found his patch on the river . . . .

Not so. But it must be said that Best had never funked a tackle. Or a barney with a yellow-card school-marm referee. He was and still, alas, is a stupendous player. Once in his last days at Old Trafford, he scored a magnificent goal. "What time did you make that?" asked a pressbox 90-minute stop-watch merchant who, in fairness, had to log these things. Said the exalting and ever perceptive David Miller of the *Express*: "Don't ask the time, mate, just confirm the date." For George Best didn't know it, but he was ever playing for our grandchildren whenever he turned it on, sleeves down, languid, lazy, arrogant.

All last winter I would see him whenever I could, playing for Fulham alongside Rodney Marsh – a mar-vellous man, but always perhaps someone playing a game for his own life. George Best was always playing a game, though he didn't twig it was for everybody's life.

Through the weeks last winter you could meet George munching his rock salmon and chips in Geales, the old world Notting Hill fish restaurant, staring into space and thinking, not alas so much on what he was going to do next Saturday as on what he had done for us before. You thought of what Derek Dougan once said: "Cruyff was made on earth, George was made in Heaven."

And you thought of the last page of Best's autobiography: "When I think about my life I keep remembering the film, *Charlie Bubbles*. Charlie is proper pissed off with everything. He finds a balloon at the bottom of his garden and just floats away. When I look into the future, I think that is how I would like to end. Floating away in a bloody great balloon with red and white stripes on it." But, actually, I did see him float away last Saturday at Craven Cottage. He had given his very best and just wandered off. Just as he reached the gate too he signed a final autograph for a friendly urchin. End all.

Guardian, 10 September 1977

BEST ANSWERS HIBERNIAN'S SOS
Patrick Barclay

Hibernian, wandering in their Scottish wilderness at the bottom of the Premier Division, yesterday signed the most unlikely saviour since Monty Python's Brian. For George Best, aged 33, and self-admittedly overweight, the Edinburgh club have agreed to pay Fulham £60,000, while Best will start receiving between £1,500 and £2,000 a match as soon as he recovers from a slight ankle injury.

He said yesterday: "I shall do my best for Hibs because they are giving me an opportunity, but if I get an approach from England I shall have to consider it."

The deal with Fulham clearly has this in mind. It provides that, should Hibernian sell Best, the London club will receive 70 per cent of any sum over £50,000, with the Scots keeping 30 per cent.

The boardroom struggle at Bristol Rovers took a new and bitter turn yesterday when Ian Stevens, the man intending to bid for control at next month's general meeting, was barred from a meeting called by six directors and a new organisation, Friends of Rovers.

Douglas Milne, a director, chaired the meeting, at which the directors publicly questioned statements made by Stevens at his own press conference earlier this week, and to say what they thought of Eastville Stadium, where they play but which they do not own.

Poor Tommy Docherty. After getting into trouble in the High Court a year ago for telling lies, he finds himself castigated by his peers for telling the truth!

Docherty's remarks to a gathering of football writers that managers sometimes cheat, tell lies, and con people were described yesterday as "disgraceful" by Jim Smith of Birmingham City.

Guardian, 17 November 1979

BEST SENT PACKING
Brian Wilson

George Best was sacked by the Scottish Premier League club Hibernian yesterday. The Hibs chairman, Tom Hart, made the announcement after his team had beaten Ayr United 2-0, without the wayward Irishman. "The marriage between Hibs and Best is over. The divorce took place at lunchtime," Hart said. "Best is available for transfer to any club in the UK, America or Canada. I told Best to pack his bags, get out and go back to London."

Best's brief career with Hibs came to an end after the wayward winger had apparently preferred a Saturday evening of revelry with Scottish rugby fans to the more restrained forms of preparation for the game.

It was the second time in eight days that Best had found himself in the dog-house and the patience of Hart finally expired. He has been guaranteeing Best his reported £2,000 a game though, in fact, the player has at least paid his way in increased gate receipts. There were 16,000 at Easter Road yesterday, in expectation of his appearance. Hibs won with goals by Lambie and McLeod.

Best trained at Easter Road all week and was fit for yesterday's match, but Hart said he was unable to rouse the former Northern Ireland star from the hotel bed where he had been staying at Hart's expense since Monday.

Best, who joined Hibs from Fulham for a £50,000 fee, was suspended by the club for failing to appear for the match against Morton on 9 February. But he apologised to the chairman and the ban was lifted.

Guardian, 18 February 1980

BEST'S DARK NIGHT
John Roberts

". . . In a real dark night of the soul it is always three o'clock in the morning, day after day." – F. Scott Fitzgerald.

At last, though far too late to save his career, it is recognised that George Best, aged 33, is not merely wayward but genuinely has a problem. Like Jimmy

Greaves before him, the most gifted footballer of his generation is an alcoholic.

Yesterday, after being sacked by the latest victim of his unreliability, Tom Hart, the chairman of Hibernian, who was reportedly paying Best £2,000 a week to play for his club, and being threatened with separation by his wife, Angie, Best found sympathisers.

Fulham, who transferred Best to Hibernian for £50,000 and who would receive 70 per cent of any fee should he be resold, offered him training facilities and an understanding smile at Craven Cottage, emphasising that they were acting on humanitarian grounds. Even more pertinent was the help offered by Alcoholics Anonymous.

As a spokesman for AA indicated: "The biggest step is admitting you are in trouble and making your mind up that you want to do something about it."

The saddening aspect, in retrospect, is that when, the day before his 26th birthday in May 1972, Best announced that he was leaving Manchester United and soccer because he was consuming a bottle of scotch a day, he was perhaps not taken seriously enough. Little more than a week later, having transferred himself from Marbella to Magaluf, Best confirmed that he would be playing for United as usual the following season.

By this time, of course, Best was finding difficulty in coping with excesses of sex, alcohol, late night gambling, media exploitation and training for football, even though he occasionally slept through an afternoon. Frank O'Farrell, his manager at United, said that during the hours he spent at the club Best was a "model professional, one of the hardest workers at training." One began to wonder what he was training for.

Dissipation was inevitable. Before long, Best again left United and effectively put a drain on his earning capacity from commercial endorsements.

His agent at the time, Ken Stanley of Huddersfield,

estimated that Best had "kicked into touch about £1 million of potential earnings from outside the game."

Best's mother died a year ago. His father, Dick, an iron turner with an electrical contractor in Belfast, discussed with me recently the question of his son's adolescence. Mr Best, who has five other children, said the family did not move to Manchester because "we didn't only have George to consider and, apart from anything else, we didn't want people thinking we were mollycoddling him."

He added: "I sometimes think I might have advised George a bit more at times, but I don't know whether it would have made any difference. We are what we are. I wonder if the average fellow would have behaved a lot differently given George's money and opportunities."

It would be grossly unfair to describe Kevin Keegan as "the average fellow." At the same time, Keegan, who was 29 last week when he announced his return from Hamburg to play for Southampton next season, has accomplished all that Best, with an infinitely superior natural talent, has failed to achieve. In terms of finance and approval, Keegan had the advantage of stubborn determination and the wit to learn from Best's mistakes. He never was the type to be trapped in a bottle.

Guardian, 19 February 1980

THE BEST WAY TO SAN JOSE
Frank Keating

By a fluke, the singer Cher (as in Sonny and) was top of the bill at Caesar's Palace when I was in Las Vegas for the fight last week. She was near me at the ringside and after Sugar Ray had done his stuff under the desert stars, the gathering of glitter – from Ali through John McEnroe to Dean Martin – twinkled inside to listen to

Cher belt out her act in the sumptuous Casino Theatre.

Out of my depth amid such heavy rollers I got to thinking – not of inconsequential matters like why a millionaire like Martin was continuing to drink from a plastic beaker, why McEnroe kept picking at the turned-up collar of his expensive suit like it was a tennis shirt, or even how quaint it would be to see the start of a letter to Cher from a Frenchman . . . No, I got to thinking about George Best.

George Best, for heaven's sake! Okay, I'll tell you. A year ago the finest footballer I ever saw, now the swarthy San Jose Earthquake in the No. 7 shirt, found himself at the end of a long bender and a short midnight hitch-hike ride down the Pacific Coast road to Malibu. He was looking for his wife, long-suffering, lovely Angela who, unable once again to cope with his moods and drinking, had left home. George suspected she was hiding at her friend Cher's villa in ritzy Malibu.

On his own admission, he was looking that night like a hung-over Mexican gardener. But he conned his way into the exclusive Colony estate by the ocean: Barbra Streisand's place was over the way, Neil Diamond's just up the road. Security was tight.

He camped outside. He was frightened. Easy prey for a Doberman wanting breakfast, he remembers with a shiver. Angela must come out soon. The sun came out first. "My head was throbbing and I desperately needed a drink. I had been in the same clothes for three days; they were stinking."

At last a jeep. It is driven by his beloved blonde. "When it is no more than 10 yards away, I jump out into the middle of the road. God knows what Angela must have thought: all I could see was the shock and anger on her face as she slammed on the brakes . . . This was it: the showdown . . .

"As I reached the jeep all the angry words stuck for a moment in my throat. I'd never seen someone I love look so pale and ill. Gone was the California tan and the lovely eyes: she looked beaten. I just stood looking at her while she stared blankly at me." Then the demon in him let rip. They had a screaming match on the road-side – and when he was through, the patient, saintly wife took him to wash and brush up in Cher's luxurious bathroom and give yet another go to the marriage she valued so. There was to be another couple of benders before, on 6 March this year, their son Calum was born, and dad helped deliver him, cutting the umbilical cord and releasing him into the world. "It was the greatest moment of my life."

George has not had a drink for nearly nine months now. He voluntarily entered a Los Angeles hospital and is a member of Starting Point, a group run on roughly the same lines as the Alcoholics Anonymous. "It is going to take many years. Years to get the poison alcohol out of my system; years to learn everything about myself. You can't get rid of guilts, fears and inhibitions you have been hiding for years in just a few weeks. My time in hospital was only the starting point."

So that's why, at a boxing match lit by the desert moon, I thought fondly last week of the finest foot-baller I have ever seen perform, and why a few days later I asked a friend to drive me from Los Angeles down to Pacific Palisades, where Governor Reagan used to live, and when a signpost pointed right to exclusive Malibu Colony I clenched a friendly fist in goodwill salute to George, Goodwill and Good Luck.

Actually, Bests and babe are now far away from the Hockney blue skies and waters of California and are being bombarded by the brown leaves of Britain's autumn. They are back to promote his new auto-biography *Where Do I Go From Here?* (Macdonald and Janes), written with Graeme Wright, which is very much a first division job of its type – humorous, touching and brutally honest.

It is even rude about George's previous life story by

his friend Mike Parkinson "which made out all I was interested in was jumping into bed with every girl I laid eyes on . . . which just wasn't true." But then he admits, "that wasn't really Mike's fault, whenever we worked on it I'd have a bottle or two of red wine in front of me."

The only boy in his street to pass the 11-plus, George at 35 remains a right little reader. The bigger the books the better. He says he wanted this latest effort "to read like John Fowles's *Daniel Martin*, you know, the past and present always merging into each other." He likes biographies best. He has just finished the Life of Edith Piaf.

One day, when there's time, he would really like to have a go himself at fiction. "Well, sort of Dick Francis stuff about football." Certainly he is always scribbling into an exercise book. "Like other things you've got to practise. You've got to work at it."

Last week, the day before I left for America, I knocked on the door of a pert and pretty concertina-tight terrace house just off the front at Southend-on-Sea, of all places. It is where George's parents-in-law live. A million miles away from Malibu-on-Sea.

The doorbell chimes like a xylophone. The blur of blonde through the frosted glass is Angela running upstairs to look decent. George greets you, his unshaven jowls accentuating the white smile. Would you like a cup of tea? Mum and Dad are out at work. The two boiled eggs are half-eaten in the kitchen. You have interrupted the second sitting for breakfast in the tiny room.

Calum crawls on the carpet. The nappies are on the line in the back garden. The sitting-room is so full of vases of flowers, you think they must be plastic. They aren't. Angie comes down and at one and the same time dries her hair, feeds and cuddles her baby, makes more tea and joins in the cheery chat from across the room as George curls up on the sofa and spouts.

It is good to be here, sure, but he reckons this is the first time he has said "When we go home" and realised he meant California. "Well I'm just an ordinary guy on the street there. I'm not 'the notorious boozy Best', with the gossip-mongers reporting every move."

Not only journalists. The day before, Angela and he had gone shopping in Southend. He had popped into a betting shop to get a quid on a horse called Lucknow in the 4.30 at Newton Abbot. "I wrote out my ticket and was standing in line when somebody recognised me and they started asking me for autographs. When I'd finished signing, the race had begun, so I couldn't get my money on." Lucknow won, of course.

He enjoyed his US season at San Jose as never before. He scored the Goal of the Season (beating seven men in the penalty area before slotting it home).

Certainly he would consider an offer from a British club for this winter – "but only something worthwhile, for a good team with a chance of winning something."

George is still little-boy in love with Manchester United. He still sits by himself sometimes and watches his film of the night they beat Benfica 5-1 in Lisbon on the day in 1966 when it all started and he came back to Manchester in a sombrero and they called him "the fifth Beatle." He never tires, either, of playing Real Madrid's 1960 European Cup final – "if only to see Di Stefano and Gento performing their solos at the pre-match kick-in."

He is still full of his newly-built house beside the Pacific Ocean where the sun beats down on its kidney-shaped swimming pool. A life away from Southend-on-Sea where, of an evening, he will wander down to the Conservative Club with his father-in-law for a game of snooker if there's nothing much on the telly.

And this night, to complete this tale of three cities, he and Angela were off to Belfast to do their stuff for a children's charity organised by his father . . . and they would drive down Ravenhill Road and, as he says in the book, "I'll glance quickly along Donard Street where my grand-parents used to live and we'll hurry through the barricades with a glance at Woolworths, the magical Woollies with its myriad delights which occupied this truant on cold afternoons long ago . . .

"And in the evening I will go with my father to his little sports club and sit laughing and drinking orange juice among the Catholics and the Protestants as the comedian cracks his jokes about the Pope and Ian Paisley. I will listen to their talk and see their love for me in their smiles. I am the hero home for a day. It is still my home. My family lives there. . . ."

And in the morning he might show tiny Calum in his arms the scrubby little patch of green where a 14-year-old once scored twice the day the Cregagh Under-17s beat the boys from Boyland and a youth club leader called Bob Bishop called Matt Busby in Manchester to say: "I believe I have found you a genius."

Guardian, 22 September 1981

ROYAL GEORGE
Frank Keating

George Best jailed. Through the drizzly mock gaiety of London's Christmas lights yesterday evening, the newspaper placards almost seemed pleased with themselves. Come-uppance at last. Christmas behind bars. In a way, it has taken an awesome and awful long time in coming to this.

While painful and horribly inevitable, dammit, yesterday's news still came as an awful blow, surely, to any sports lover of my generation. If the exclamation-marked banner headlines have moved steadily, almost terribly, over the last two decades from the simple joyous back pages to the snide gossip columns and now to the bald-facts front, there can have only been a few of us who abdicated the faith that George Best was the finest footballer we ever saw.

He could do everything. He stood only so-high and ran out looking as frail and lonely as a corner-flag, a waif who'd missed his breakfast, his chapped fingers tugging the long-red sleeves for warmth.

Then somebody – Law, Crerand, Stiles or Charlton – gave him the ball. He could embroider mesmerising patterns in front of any defence: the tougher the cheating, the more he would antagonise and make us laugh. He could pass generously and to the instinctive inch. He was at one and the same time inventive and dainty, carefree and competitive, ruthless, brave and chivalrous: he would dance into forays where angels feared, and he had the shot of an Antrim mule.

Only a couple of weekends ago a friend some 20 years younger than I offered the Dutchman, Johann Cruyff, as a more complete footballer. Pelé and possibly Puskas, I supposed. Tom Finney? But Cruyff? Total football might be one thing but a total footballer was another.

"Bestie," Paddy Crerand said, "was a Finney, greater by far than Matthews." Bobby Charlton, who was not enamoured overmuch with George's life style in the clubs, nevertheless gives Best – "George could do anything with the ball: when he was with us in the early days he was simply magical and breathtaking."

Best, clean-shaven and in the trim, unburdened by the spirits, was a delightful, intelligent companion. Every year he did his best about his alcoholism. For 10 years now he has been in and out of clinics. Even as he was arrested this time he had, apparently, a stomach implant to help kick the habit.

A couple of years ago I went to see him at his then in-laws' little concertina type of terrace house just off the front at Southend-on-Sea. He told me that morning, playing with his son, Calum, when he was being supported and loved by his wife, Angie, that his alcoholism "was going to take many years to get over, to get the poison out of my system, to get rid of guilts, fears and inhibitions I have been hiding for years."

The night before Manchester United had been on the television. He was rivetingly good about discussing the match. He told me how, sometimes, however low or high, he still switched on the video and watched film of the night they beat Benfica 5-1 in Lisbon in 1966 when it all started – or when Real Madrid won the European final in 1960 – "I always watch that first few minutes just to see Di Stefano and Gento performing their solo wizardry at the pre-match kick-in."

Three or four weeks ago a public-relations officer rang me from Reading. A sponsor was arranging a gala match at Elm Park – Reading against New Zealand. The bait was that George Best would be playing. Sorry, I said, I was going to Ireland with the rugby Australians. And there, after the match at Belfast's Ravenhill, a friend walked with me through the neighbouring tidy trim estate and we made a diversion for him to point out where George had first kicked a ball, a stubby little patch of green where a 14-year-old once scored twice the day the Cregagh under-17s beat the boys from Boyland and Bob Bishop sent a telegram to Matt Busby about his genius.

He had also been the only boy in that street to pass the 11-plus. But just those four years later the telegram was acted on and Busby brought him to Manchester's singing, seedy, swinging 60s . . .

A TALE OF TWO SENTENCES
Editorial

As the prison door closed upon them this week, George Best faces one Christmas behind bars, while Colin Evans, the murderer of four-year-old Marie Payne, faces at least 30. The two cases, different in the extreme, are a reminder that, under Mr Leon Brittan's Home Office regime, prison sentencing comes tough at both ends of the spectrum.

The Evans case has exposed serious professional failings in several parts of the social service and criminal justice systems. Few, though, will disagree that Evans, with his prolonged and horrible record of child abuse, must be kept firmly in a locked institution. The life sentence dished out by Mr Justice Jones was both mandatory and justified. But Evans still spotlights an unresolved issue in penal policy. Mr Brittan has nailed his political colours to long sentences for violent crime. He has said he will not consider parole or release on licence for such criminals until they have served at least 20 years – or more in some cases, presumably including that of Evans. It is a policy which literally stores up problems. First, the proportion of the prison population serving long sentences will grow, and is already doing so. This means providing more long-stay prisons, for which Mr Brittan has obtained Treasury backing. But how many prisons is enough? Second, prison staff need clearer guidance about what they are supposed to do with no-hope prisoners. The hard line may be the right line, but it destroys the meaning of rehabilitative regimes, especially for lifers. There are no votes to be won solving the problem, yet prison warders, medical staff and social workers, not to mention prisoners themselves, have a right to know what is expected from them. By the time that the 75-year-old Colin Evans becomes eligible for release on licence in 2014, perhaps then the 75-year-old Lord Brittan of Richmond will have come up with a few suggestions.

George Best's fate highlights a more immediate and widespread problem. In Best's case, the judge called his three-month sentence for drunk driving and assault "neither excessive nor unduly severe." Nevertheless there is a suspicion that Best is being treated in this way at least partly because he is famous. There is a whiff of sanctimoniousness about the whole thing. You are an idol, Mr Best, who has abused idle pleasures, and you are to be punished for our misjudgement. But is prison really the right place for George Best? Will it do any good for anyone other than the Pentonville First XI? George Best's problem is that he drinks too much. So do many, very many, other people. Save in a very small minority of cases, the criminal justice system has no answers for either the railway arch wino or the Champagne Charlie. The country, and George Best, need a pro-active not a reactive alcohol policy, as yesterday's Labour Party report, *Cold Comfort*, argues.

The danger – from Best to Evans – is in seeing the sentence alone as some sort of a bottom line drawn by society. It isn't, and can't be. Sentencing is but one aspect of a total policy. You can, as the Appeal Court has indeed done both last week and this week, sentence well-known gossip columnists and film actors to prison sentences for carrying personal supplies of cocaine into the country. But every jot of evidence in such matters points to the unpalatable fact that it is the certainty of detection – that is the cuts-depleted customs' infrastructure – which deters, and not the well-publicised delivery of heavy sentences and heavy judicial sentiments. Mr Brittan wanted a coherent policy but, as ever, the balance seems to elude him in practice. It is easy to take a serious case, deal out a serious sentence, and forget; it is very hard to take the far less serious and see a punishment which more sentiently fits the crime.

Guardian, 19 December 1984

TV COMPANIES RISK BEST ACTION REPLAY DESPITE FOUL ON *WOGAN*
Dennis Barker

George Best's explicit interview on the *Wogan* show may have put the BBC's switchboards under siege from irate viewers but it has failed to deter other television companies.

While the BBC was "looking into every aspect" of the interview, Sky News and London Weekend Television were welcoming the unpredictable footballer into their studios.

Best last night appeared with Frank Bough on Sky News and was due to record another interview for Gloria Hunniford's LWT programme, *Sunday, Sunday.*

Both seemed undaunted by the prospect. On Sky, Bough carefully led him through an interview during which Best occasionally asked permission for an expletive which was duly granted.

LWT said it had had no second thoughts about bringing in Best.

Some might say that anyone who invites Best deserves all he gets. Terry Wogan certainly got it on the live programme, when the heavy-drinking former football star spoke somewhat too frankly.

Best, 44-year-old Northern Irishman, once given three months for drunk driving, replied when Wogan asked him about his womanising: "I like screwing, right?"

Asked what he did with his time now, he replied: "Screw." He added that the press were "arseholes", and that football managers talked "shit".

Yesterday he was unrepentant as he left his Chelsea flat to find a bunch of "arseholes" outside his door. He warned a persistent questioner: "You behave yourself, or I will give you a smack in the face."

But although it seemed as if he were after some kind of profanity record, a trace of caution remained: when called upon to give his opinion of Terry Wogan, he uncharacteristically but wisely (for a man out to publicise the latest book about him, *The Good, The Bad and The Bubbly*) declined.

All of which is genuinely, tragically sad for those who remember Best as a 15-year-old Manchester United apprentice who within six years was ranked as the finest footballer in Britain and then in Europe.

But the pressures weighed on a man still in many ways the boy who left United after a fortnight because he was homesick and had to be talked back by his shipbuilder father.

His past has included receiving 10,000 fan letters a week, consuming four bottles of champagne as a social drink, going on benders lasting up to 26 days, heavy gambling, "screwing" up to seven women a day, and going bankrupt with a tax bill that has risen to £43,000 with interest.

Best, who spends much of his time coaching children, is shortly off on a speaking tour of the US. One in Australia was curtailed this year after he failed to turn up at three engagements. Best can still shock, but he can hardly surprise.

Guardian, 21 September 1990

THE BILLEN INTERVIEW
Andrew Billen

Outside the Phene Arms in Chelsea, Jane Bown has plonked George Best on a moulded plastic chair and is trying to impel some life into his eyes, which have been pied by an afternoon's residence in the pub. Best does what he can by hollering at passing women to "do him a favour" by joining him on his knee. Although some of these girls are too young to be quite sure who this grey-bearded inebriate with dandruff over his "Legend" bomber jacket is, none actually turns the invitation down. Yet even as he pecks at them, his grey-blue eyes refuse to gleam and only dim further when a half-pint glass of white wine arrives in the hand of the most flagrantly talented footballer of our time.

The Best I am charged with interviewing this evening has little in common with the Best I have been reading about in his new collection of soccer apocrypha, *The Best of Times* (Simon and Schuster). The book gives us chirpy versions of both the game's history and Best's. In the way that one volume of his autobiography was flippantly titled *The Good, The Bad and The Bubbly*, the new chapter on his alcoholism is chummily headed "Cheers!" In it he assures us that his drinking is under control and gives due credit to Mary Shatila, "my common-law wife, my lover and best friend, my confidante and my strength".

There is many a slip, however, and since writing the book Best has suffered what the police would call a bit of a domestic. Six weeks ago he announced that he had fallen in love with a 22-year-old air hostess called Alex Pursey and that, after only four days together, they were planning a new life in Los Angeles. But the course of true love ne'er did run smooth and the pair were soon falling out over claims Best had made to the *News Of The World*, which he subsequently admitted were false. As a result the paper withdrew the £15,000 they had offered Best for the tale.

Had he, I ask, when we retire inside, really fallen in love?

"Oh that was true," he says in the only Ulster accent I have ever heard that could be called warm. "But I warned her: 'You are going around with somebody the media is very interested in.' And she said: 'I've been through it.' And I said: 'What are you talking about?' And she said: 'With John.' And I said: 'With John

Scales! From Wimbledon! It's a bit different!' And then it wasn't funny any more. The press were camped outside her door, my door, her mother's door. Her parents called me – they were all right, funnily enough.

"Denis Law phoned me and said: 'What are you doing?' And Denis is my best pal, he really is. He said: 'You are 48. She's 22.' And I said: 'Denis, it really doesn't bother me.'"

But on this evening's performance, Best's love life is far more complicated than the tabloids have allowed. His admiration for Mary, who still shares his home and indeed, against some odds, set up this interview, remains. "She's in a different class," he says. "She is a very special woman. But you don't get up in the morning and say: 'I'm going to meet this 22-year-old and fall madly in love.' I am trying to explain that to her."

How are the expectations going?

"They aren't working," he chuckles. "No, she has been so understanding but in the last couple of years things haven't been right for us. I was faithful to Mary for seven years but I said I was going to do my own thing and she should do hers. So now she checks the numbers every night to see where I am."

The numbers in his little black book?

"It's not little," he says.

At this point we are joined by a well-presented woman called Tania, who says, in a voice I last heard emerging from Mandy Smith's lips, that she plans to marry Best in Vegas. What would we all like to drink?

As Tania makes for the bar, Best points out to me a blonde who is looking daggers at him from another corner of the Phene. "I'm taking her to a health farm at the weekend," he boasts. "I get away with murder. I really do. But, I mean, they're not exactly ugly are they?"

Tania returns and snuggles up against the legend, who absently caresses her nose. What is it about him?

"Everything, I suppose," she says unhelpfully. "He is very unique, a bit different from your average man. I stayed up till midnight reading his book, the Bubbly one. It was better than *EastEnders*, and *EastEnders* is my favourite programme. I hadn't realised what you had been through, George."

Best and I are just getting into a discussion of what he has been through – a forest of difficulties that included divorce, bankruptcy and a three-month jail sentence – when a bloke lurches up to Jane and puzzlingly says that he is waiting for her apology. As the enormity of this affront dawns on Best, things get rather exciting.

"George: no," says Tania, who has a "deal" that there is no fighting when they are out together. It is agreed that the landlord rather than Best should approach the belligerent. "Could you very tactfully tell him," says Best, "that unless he apologises I'll tear his fucking head off?"

When the publican returns with the news that there has been a genuine misunderstanding, Best is grudgingly placated. "He is," he says, "a very lucky man. To insult you in front of me is very, very dangerous."

But he is not a violent man, I say. I mean, he has never been convicted for violence.

"Only four times," says Best. "But nothing serious. I sit in the corner and don't bother anyone. But I get so many arseholes coming at me I have actually gone the other way. I love it now. I know I can beat anyone. I say: 'Go on. Do it then.'"

I wonder if he would find himself in fewer scrapes, romantic and combative, if he did not drink so much.

"But," says Tania, "I don't think he does drink too much. We go out and I'm a faster drinker than him, aren't I? Hint, hint! I've known alcoholics in my life and George is not an alcoholic."

"No, I am," says Best.

"You've a drink problem but you are not an alcoholic," Tania insists.

Best's mother drank herself to death 16 years ago. "It really pissed me off," he says. "I thought it was my fault. I was in LA at the time and I had to come back for the funeral. It really pissed me off."

He stops himself, aware that this is not coming out as he intends. "Actually, it didn't piss me off: it upset me. I thought it was me who did it to her because of all the shit I had been through. It really freaked me out. I used to go to hotels and get close to killing myself with drink. And the guilt still goes on, to a certain degree."

People were writing off Best's life as a cautionary tale even before it started to unravel. In a gloomy television profile by Hugh McIlvanney in the 1960s even Best, at the height of his success, mourned: "Football is a very sad sport. It's the only thing I've been able to do since I was 15 and when you get to 30 you must think you are on the way out." Yet talk of his tragedy has surely been overdone. As he says: "Over the last few years I've lost a lot of friends at a very young age and I was the one who they kept saying wouldn't make 30, wouldn't make 40, wouldn't make 50: and I'm still here."

But you need not be the kind of melancholic commentator our national game seems to produce to be moved by Best, especially when he tells you for the nth time that he doesn't care why women want him. "Print this," he says sententiously: "I Don't Give A Shit." This, remarks Tania, is his favourite saying. It is poignant for, in many ways, he obviously still does.

Guardian, 2 October 1994

MAN WITH A LOT OF BOTTLE
Emma Lindsey

There once was a ditty, "Georgie Best, superstar, walks like a woman and wears a bra." Granted it didn't say much about the greatest talent British football ever produced, but it trumpeted the ubiquity of his magnificence right down to the playground. Whether or not you're old enough to remember seeing the double-jointed genius score his 137 goals in 361 League games, the living legend staggers on in the memory.

Quietly slipping into the function room of the Phene Arms in London's Chelsea, nodding and winking shyly at the assembly, he still seems befuddled, after all these years, by the fame which stalks before him.

"The British have a great knack of making super-stars out of losers," he says, bemused and shrugging. "It's a hell of a compliment to think I haven't played for 25 years and I'm busier now than I've ever been. I'm just a kid from Belfast."

Hardly. Still, one wonders just how long can a man milk a football career that ended a quarter of a century ago? Besty might join you in a ponder, doubtless over a couple of pints of wine.

The video, *Drugs, Mugs and Thugs* (BMG Video), is the latest in a long line of football memorabilia. Boasting the lowdown on the high points of the '94–'95 football season, it has two–blokes–down–the–pub cosi-ness as Best and Rodney Marsh chew the scratchings. On Andy Cole's transfer deal: "I think the money's gone nuts. For that you'd want 40 goals a season." On Kung-fu Cantona: "I'm amazed that what happened with Eric doesn't happen more often. Sooner or later somebody was going to get chinned."

Vintage stuff from a man who knows his grapes. On Paul Merson's unfortunate little habits: "I think it was sad he had to stand up and admit it. It's the greatest lifestyle in the world, being a footballer. You can't beat it. You're getting paid to travel the world, keep fit, with people hounding you for autographs. Why would you jeopardise it?"

Good question from someone who has undergone enforced self-analysis within the confines of drying-out clinics. In his earlier autobiography, *The Good, The Bad and The Bubbly*, he talks with affecting candour about his downward spiritual spiral. But none of it, not the threats, counselling or the alcohol-deterrent drugs implanted with horrific complications in his stomach, had much effect. Years later he may have lost some rocket power and startling good looks but he still seems on a mission to self-destruct.

"I've got away with a lot more than other people could," he chuckles. With the same understatement he mulls over the latest crop of talent: "Newcastle's Ginola looks class and Ruud Gullit seems a breath of fresh air. Then there's the lad Yeboah. There's some good players about but we don't have any world class. Gazza is a good player but not world class. I don't think at the end of the day anyone is going to turn around and say he was great."

The booze, birds and scandal – all have done their job better than the most diligent PR ever could to keep him in the headlines. Pausing to flick dandruff off his navy jumper, the 49-year-old takes another slurp from his refill.

"I still miss being with the boys. When football's been part of your life since you were 15, it's a big loss. It's difficult. A lot of players get into trouble because they are looking for something to give them a buzz.

"I've found mine at last through working on Sky, doing the roadshow with Rodney and radio, being in front of the public and getting a reaction. You get good days and bad days. But it's like a game. If you have a bad one, you can't wait till the next one to prove yourself and put it behind you."

A philosophy he has applied to his love life, which has proved to be a veritable conveyor belt of women.

The latest is blonde, slender, 23-year-old Alex. Tanned after a week in Portugal, the former Virgin Atlantic air hostess has turned up to stand by her man. They wed in July, though it was touch and go when Alex changed her mind after one of Besty's benders.

Two months later, he's still in love and tweaks her chin in greeting. "All right, Besty, all right, Besty," she coos in reply, kissing his nose. It would make a bizarre spectacle: she in black leather trousers and high-heeled boots, he in well-worn slacks, except that it fits too well into the crazy travelling show that is his life.

"Alex is a beautiful woman," he says, with a bleary wink across the room. "She could have chosen anyone she wanted. I don't know why she chose me. We didn't plan to fall in love, it just happened."

Like the well-documented bankruptcy, satyriasis and imprisonment. As a helping hand places yet another half-pint tipple by his feet, he ruminates: "Players are bigger today because for some strange reason they think they have to be big to be tough. But when you look back at the bad boys, Dave Mackay, Chopper Harris, Nobby Stiles, they were all midgets."

Perhaps the answer to the decline of football's best lies in a hall of mirrors. When he walked away too soon from the game he loved, the man whom Pelé called the greatest footballer in the world must have looked too small in his own eyes, overshadowed by personal demons.

Observer, 24 September 1995

SWINGER NOTCHES HIS HALF-CENTURY
Frank Keating

George Best is 50 on Wednesday. When British football's most gifted superstar – and star-crossed rapscallion – walked away from the game at 27 with a bottle under one arm and a bevy of blondes on the other, he was told he would be lucky to reach 30.

When he was 38 and incarcerated in Pentonville jail after failing to appear in court on a drink-driving charge, they said he would not make 40.

As he clocks up his half-century – "honestly, I might not have a drink to celebrate the day if the mood's not upon me; then again, y'know, I might" – Best remains on the top-most plinth in the hall of fame.

For breathtaking range he is ahead of Matthews, Finney, Greaves, Charlton, Law, Gallacher, Baxter and Charles, and even though he danced in the green only fitfully on the world stage he probably runs Pelé closer than Puskas, Di Stefano, Cruyff and Maradona.

If the deserved fame of this tubby middle-aged man, the glint of mischief still in his dark eyes if no longer in his ankles, bestrides the century, his time bridges the chasm of the two-part history of British football.

You know he was born to Ann, wife of a shipyard-worker Dick, in the Belfast Royal maternity hospital on 22 May 1946. When you look up other dates it is hard not to whistle a "phew" – for on his 15th birthday he joined Manchester United, the very summer of 1961 that Jimmy Hill and Cliff Lloyd of the Professional Footballers' Association celebrated the abolition of the maximum wage.

Two birthdays later Best signed as a professional at Old Trafford and between then and playing his first League game in red against West Brom on 14 September 1963, Mr Justice Wilberforce had, in the High Court in July, pronounced to George Eastham an end to the "retain and transfer" system.

At a stroke the feudal fields were laid to waste – and a 17-year-old sprite was setting them on fire. English soccer was not remotely prepared. It could not cope. Finney was still playing for Preston, and working as a plumber in his summers, Matthews was still catching the bus to training at Stoke – but it was the Swinging Sixties, and the Ulster sprig found himself with unlimited money and a white Jaguar (with L-plates) and they called him the fifth Beatle.

Best ruminates, although with no hint of blame nor regret: "Nobody could protect me, advise me. They didn't know how to. It hadn't happened to a footballer before." Today even half-mediocre players are surrounded by agents, bankers and bouncers; they no longer live in mock-Tudor mansions but in Grade 1 Tudor mansions.

"Now every footballer is protected. Of course it was a problem for me. All of a sudden I had to employ three full-time secretaries just to answer the 10,000 letters a week. At the time I thought it happened to every footballer.

"I wasn't protected because it hadn't happened before in English football. There was no precedent. I was being asked for more photo-calls in pop magazines than sports ones."

The whole crazy stir and blur are examined on television tomorrow night when, to raise a glass to the famous 50th, BBC 2 performs another of its occasional streaks of brilliance by giving over half the evening schedule to Best.

There is a frank, almost haunting, interview by Michael Parkinson (don't fret, it is taped, George turns up) and much fun and games and goals and goals . . .

There is the inevitable competition to choose Best's bestest – but he was far, far more than a goalscorer, though 179 for United in 466 matches was phenomenal for an "out" player who never had the specialist strikers' roll-ins.

Early on, doubtless, will be the brace against Benfica in the Stadium of Light all of 30 springtimes ago when the 19-year-old announced himself to the whole world. Surely they will end with the very last, for the San Jose Earthquakes in 1980 when he beat seven men inside the penalty area before slippering the ball home.

But were the cameras there for his last in England, in 1977 when he signed off for Fulham on a skid-pan pitch with an exquisite lob which kissed the crossbar and fell over the line with Oldham's poor goalie on his backside?

That aptly put his signature on the glory of his British career (after it he played 17 woebegone games for Hibernian and five for Bournemouth). I suppose his last competitive game in England was for the Ford Open Prison XI after his transfer from Pentonville in the 1984–85 season. If he got a game, that is.

When he arrived in the Black Maria, the prison team's coach Malcolm Holman said: "Whether he's George Best or Pelé, he won't get a look-in in this squad unless he's prepared to train."

Nowadays Best recalls, with no malice but a sigh: "When I was an apprentice at 15 I was in the stand when Real Madrid came to Old Trafford. At the kick-in the Spanish goalie rolled the ball out to Gento, the veteran winger. He shot it back with his left foot – but he put a vicious back-spin on it so the well-struck ball took one bounce and at once skidded back to him.

"I was mesmerised. 'Wow, I must try that.' I spent the next months working non-stop on my left foot. In the end it became even better than my natural right. Bobby [Charlton] had done the same – he worked so hard at it that many of his great goals came from his left."

Best is still bearded like the pard but suddenly much more grey. His fingernails still, as they ever did, pick at his jowls shyly during an interview. They did when he was the fifth Beatle and they did when I spent a day with him as he was living and lying low with his then in-laws at Southend-on-Sea in a terraced house off the front.

He was on the wagon; button-bright, which he remains. He had knocked off half the *Telegraph* crossword and asked if the *Guardian*'s was more challenging. He brewed the tea, chewing over football, then we went to the betting shop: a nag called Lucknow was a cert in the 2.30 at Newton Abbot.

He wrote out his ticket and stood in the queue. Somebody recognised him. Autograph-slips came in from the whole shop, the street and beyond. He signed each one but missed his place in the queue. No bet. Lucknow walked it at 15-1. The brief episode was enough to turn any sane man to drink.

Some of his one-time casino bets make your hair curl. He has walked away from the serious tables – "lose 10 quid now and I'm a mess." He admits he was an alcoholic all right – "booze controlled me totally" – but now he drinks some days and others not at all.

His second wife, 25-year-old Alex – "she knows I've loved 2,000 women but only been in love this once" – is obviously a true brick as well as truly beautiful. "What a compliment that she's willing to share a life with me."

On tomorrow's film his American born-and-bred son Calum pledges troth. A handsome (although blonde through Best's first wife Angie) teenager, Calum "quite likes this soccer game of dad's". And meanwhile the old man picks at his beard and chuckles: "The bottom line is that I'm still enjoying life enormously."

George Best 50 and full of the joys? There is hope, thank him and heaven, for all of us.

Guardian, 2 May 1996

GRIZZLED GENIUS
Sabine Durrant

The current Mrs George Best, a 26-year-old former air hostess, is standing on the sidelines watching her husband do what he does best. They run up to him, they pass it to him and he's off with it. The dexterity! The speed! No one can touch him. It's in! It's a signature! And another! And another! "I support Chelsea," Alex Best tells me, "although I don't think I could watch a match through to the end."

We're in a bookshop in Oxford Street and George, casual in a white Aertex top and blue Umbro trousers, is signing copies of his latest authorised biography. "All right. Cheers," he says about 200 times, though when an elderly woman who has queued for an hour wants to describe how, all those years ago, his face and legs decorated her son's bedroom walls, he leans forward sweetly to catch every word and then chortles "Poor you." They've brought their Instamatics, too, and again and again he grins that swollen-lower-lip grin, leaning into the lens alongside the old men, the young women, the Japanese tourists, the student in the Liverpool shirt ("This is the best thing that has happened to me in three years at university"), the mums, the dads, the kids.

A little girl of about eight keeps sliding up under the rails: "Georgie, where did you get that?" she says, nodding at a copy of the book. And then later, "Georgie, where did you get that?" pointing at his glass of white wine.

He gets it from his wife, whose job it is to keep it filled. ("Alex," he calls in some panic every 15 minutes or so, flicking his head towards his empty glass.) She's pin thin with long cream hair and very brown skin. She says it's from the garden but there are suspicious orange marks between her fingers. She's wearing buttock-tight white jeans, high gold shoes and a

camouflage print singlet. She's standing by the "How
To" shelves and occasionally spots a title that takes her
interest. "Bluff your way in Tax!" she says. "That would
be a good one." "The Management Guide to Understanding Behaviour – ah!" She likes Jilly Cooper –
Rivals and *Riders*, though not her most recent "which
was rubbish." "Bless," she says when she hears the
eight-year-old girl.

It's a relief all round that George has turned up. He
has a habit of "going on the missing list" as he puts it.
He's missed training sessions; he's missed matches; he's
missed his own birthday parties; in 1995 he even
missed his first scheduled wedding to Alex ("He has
been on a two-week bender and has turned into a
monster," she told the *Sun* at the time – although she
forgave him enough to marry him two weeks later).
He's also done bunks in the middle of interviews, which
is why I abandoned a plan to talk to him somewhere
more salubrious and, when the public signing was over,
secured him in a backroom of the bookshop. No
windows. An alarm on the door.

So there he is, sitting on a stained office chair,
surrounded by empty boxes and remaindered books: the
man who in the sixties and early seventies was arguably
the greatest, the most glamorous, footballer in the
world. He was "the fifth Beatle", the first dribbling
superstar, the young Ulsterman who arrived at
Manchester United at the age of 15, eight stone and
crying with homesickness every night, who learned to
play like a god on the pitch and a devil off it. For when
there wasn't the football, there were the boutiques
("George Best Rogue" of Manchester) and the night
clubs (he opened a den called Slack Alice), the gambling,
the birds (the actresses, the bevy of Miss Worlds) – and
the booze. "But through all those sorts of things," he
says to me in his high, tight voice with its soft Northern
Irish accent, "all I wanted to do was kick a ball around."

Hugh McIlvanney, the sports writer, once said that

"sport at its finest is often poignant, if only because it is almost a caricature of the ephemerality of human achievements." And the tragedy of a great footballer is how long they have to live after the talent has gone, how many careers they have to go through, how many times they have to recreate themselves.

Michael Parkinson, an old friend, said at the time of the cataclysmic *Wogan* interview in 1990 (in which Best dissolved into a swearing, boorish drunk), that he thought the drinking began with boredom. And how boring life must have seemed for so long to Best. During our interview, he continues signing books, which the wife who never saw him play passes to him, and he stops and looks me in the face only a few times. One of these times is when he's describing what it was like to fire a huge crowd. "It's just being able to do something that you find so easy in front of 60 or 70,000 people every week and you know that you're better than anybody else and you can do what you want. It's . . . I mean, it's just . . . total . . . adrenalin is exactly right. I used to think, this is heaven."

He's sober today, articulate for the first half hour, but very wheezy after that, his breathing coming in noisy stops and starts. That great mane of black hair is thin and grey enough now to start looking greasy and his beard, which Alex trims for him, is almost white. But his eyebrows, little surprised darts, are still black as sin and he has the same Chaucerian gap between his two front teeth. He is quite portly.

"My weight's up and down and my knee's a bit of a mess. We go to a health farm at Henlow Grange but if I go on the machine for an hour running, going up stairs is a problem because the knee is shattered. Some nights if we've been out, or if we've been flying, it swells up really badly. Bestie [which is what he and Alex call each other] gives me a massage. She gives me a facial. She looks after my hair. I'm just a lazy bugger."

"And I cut your beard," adds Alex. "When we first

got married I made him shave it all, but actually now I prefer it stubbly."

The couple live what they are keen to insist is a glamorous lifestyle. Best has his own wine label, a column in *Punch* and "I have my own magazine, *George Best United Monthly*," and does work for Sky. But the bulk of his income comes from public speaking. Alex accompanies him everywhere as his personal assistant. "The after dinner circuit is massive, it really is," he says. "In the couple of years we've been together, work-wise we've been to New Zealand, Malaysia, Portugal, Hong Kong. All paid for. Staying in the best hotels in the world."

Do they travel first class? "That's the first thing we say," answers Best quickly. "It makes me laugh when I pick up the papers and they talk about, you know, 'wasted'; it makes me laugh when I see 'fallen idol', or 'fallen legend'. I think these people who are writing it are sitting in an office nine to five and I don't know what they earn, but I'm going out and getting paid sometimes £5,000 for an interview! And I'm thinking, who's fallen here? And if I wanted to earn more I could earn double!"

The Bests have had a tricky few months because of a legal row involving George's former agent, Bill McMurdo, and the Chelsea flat in which George has lived for the past 14 years. But things were settled last week, money changed hands, and they've put an offer on another flat facing Albert Bridge.

"We're under oath not to talk about it," says Alex. "I've just said we're moving," snaps George, in the one moment of tension between them.

When Alex moved into the original flat, she went round it with a decorator – "the carpet was disgusting" – and painted the walls pink. "Soft pink with a darker pink ceiling." She loves DIY and will be sad to leave the stencilling she did on the kitchen cupboards. But she's glad to have a fresh start, without the memories of the other women who've lived or slept there. She gets on well with Angie, the first Mrs Best and mother of George's son Calum (now aged 17), who was a witness in the court case. "Angie keeps telling me what to eat and what not to eat," says George. "I said: 'Angela, I'm 52. It's a bit late.'" Alex seems at ease with her womaniser husband, but when she tells me how much she loved *Bridget Jones's Diary* the bit she picks out is "when she's in the flat and she knows, she just knows, he's got another woman there and she's looking in all the odd places. I really laughed at that."

When the Bests talk about their life together – sybaritic as it may be – you get the impression of two people killing time. They love crosswords: "We're hooked. We're hooked," says Alex. "We start off easy," explains George. "Alex does the quickie and I'll do the quiz words in the morning and then in the afternoon we do the cryptics and we just drive ourselves nuts. All my close friends are into quizzes.

"Denis Law is a great friend and sometimes we'll go on flights on a plane for 12 hours and it's just 12 hours of him trying to out-do me and me trying to out-do him." George reads a lot of true crime, Alex reads recipe books. "Pies. Steak and Kidney. Lasagne. I try things out on you, don't I, George?" Does she even make her own pastry? "She makes everything," says her husband with an edge of pride.

He doesn't eat in the day; just white wine at lunch, but he likes a meal, preferably a Chinese, around five. They prefer to go to the same handful of restaurants (Harrods Oyster Bar is their favourite), and the same few pubs, particularly their local, the Phene Arms in Chelsea. Alex drives. George has surrendered the wheel (he used to be addicted to white Jaguars) and has given her a black BMW. Personalised number plate: E8 ALEX. "E8 doesn't mean anything. We wanted E11 for the number on his shirt," says Alex. "But they wanted another 20 grand for it," says George.

They go to Tramp still, where they first met, and on Friday they were spending his 52nd birthday at the Palm Beach casino in Berkeley Square. "You get a nice meal there," says Alex.

Best has always liked to go to places where he's known. He says it's because he gets into trouble if he strays. "We still get the idiots coming up. We get into arguments because I won't walk away from it. But I figure if someone comes up and insults me and my wife, I'm entitled to do something about it. Well, the latest one who came up wanted to know who the bimbo was . . . " He laughs through his teeth. "So she started and I'm like freaking out, so we ended up having an argument because I wouldn't back down.

"You get that once in a while, it's guys trying to be flash in front of their girlfriends or wives or pals. They never do it when they're on their own, funnily enough." And why does he think he attracts them? "Jealousy. That's the word. It's jealousy. Otherwise there's no reason for it."

"We're just sitting having a quiet drink or a nice meal," says Alex. "Then the nice meal's ruined." So he really doesn't provoke it? There have, after all, been the occasional headlines since he married Alex. ("Best beat me up says wife", that sort of thing.) "I have a drink when I feel like it – as simple as that. If I don't feel like it I don't and if I've had enough I go to bed. I can't remember the last time I got seriously drunk. I've not had a hangover for years."

"It's normally me now you have to put to bed," giggles Alex. "We both enjoy ourselves, we both like a glass of wine . . ." continues George. "You had to take me home after the court case . . . Afterwards I mean, it was the relief," explains Alex.

All this time, Best has been signing books. But he has begun to slow down; Alex is holding the next one out and he's not taking it. I asked if he thought much about the past, if he had regrets?

He looked irritated. "Nah, I don't think so. I've been through things I'd rather not go through. Nobody wants to go to prison. I did. I've been in hospital twice, no three times. I've had implants to stop me drinking which were disastrous. All that stuff, I suppose."

Does he wish he came from anything other than Northern Ireland and could have played serious football internationally? "I've always believed that's the way it is. No good thinking about it. It wasn't to be so . . ." But he's still bitter that Manchester United never awarded him a testimonial. "That's one thing that really bugs me."

And he still feels bad about his mother, who died an alcoholic. "It hit me really hard, because you think could you have done more? If I'd been there, could it have been different? You know, at first I wrote, three, four times a week, but then you grow up and you drift away . . . You've got your own lifestyle and . . . But for a long time I felt a lot of guilt. It was like a millstone. But I realise I wouldn't have made any difference." Did he ever talk about his own addiction with her? "Yes, but luckily she went before I had my serious problems – I think that would have been worse for her."

There is something very sad at the centre of Best. He says he's a "big kid" and in many ways that's how he seems. He likes to live in a present in which all is well – his father lives in Belfast, but he won't talk about the Troubles; it's as if he won't let that sort of thing touch him.

When things go wrong in his life, it's nothing to do with him: "There are a lot of crazy people out there!" He likes to tell you stories about things he's supposed to have done – "But I wasn't even in the country!" And again and again, this man who many believe threw it all away before he fulfilled his true potential when he retired from top-flight football at 27, seems to want to prove to himself how much he's worth, how much he means to people.

There's the time he met Eric Clapton, who went out of his way specially; the things his manager and mentor Sir Matt Busby said about him. And there's the time the fifth Beatle met Paul McCartney. "I used to bump into Ringo at Tramp quite a bit," he recalls. "And once I was in there and Paul McCartney was in having a drink with Linda. He waved and I waved back and when they were leaving, Linda came up behind me and just whispered in my ear: 'We love you.' She just whispered it. It was all she said. We love you. It just freaked me out, it really did." For a moment, he looks as though he is about to cry. But then he seems to notice his wife, 26 and beautiful, beside him. She hands him a book. He gets back to business. "Are you sure these are all 'Best Wishes'?" he asks.

Guardian, 25 May 1998

YESTERDAY IN BELFAST, THE MOST POIGNANT SADNESS
Michael Walker

Back where it all began the snow crunched underfoot around Belfast's Cregagh estate yesterday morning. Lowry-like figures hugged themselves against the worst as they made their way to and from the shops on Greenway, where Mawhinney's the butcher proclaims "Meat to please you" and where the flags and murals shout of Ulster loyalism. Down on Burren Way, where the Cregagh's most famous resident used to practise with a tennis ball against his parents' doorknob, the waiting went on. Then at lunchtime, the end: George Best was dead.

There was no ceremony. Best had not lived in this sprawling 1940s housing estate for nearly half a century. Yet to those of us who grew up in this corner of Belfast it always felt as if George, always just George, maintained a presence. We wallowed in the warmth of his golden shadow. Yesterday was cold, tearful, distressing, but when Belfast regains composure it will be to say that he was one of us, always will be. It will be to say they can take his body away but that George Best will never die.

You cannot bury a legend and, since the day in December 1972 when Best played his last match for Manchester United, that is what he has been, a beautiful, living football memory. There were moments after that when he rekindled the flame – notably for Northern Ireland against Johann Cruyff's Holland in 1976 – but Best the meaningful footballer finished in 1972. From there his career, his life, was drowned in drink and we cannot forget the pain he inflicted verbally and physically when in thrall to alcohol, not least on his family.

Belfast is not a city noted for forgiveness but where George Best was concerned, among the public, it was a bottomless well. To local politicians it was different, though of course now there is a notion that the proposed new national stadium should be named after Best. It's too late.

It should have been done years ago. Unofficially Best must have known what he meant to Belfast, but it would have been good for him to see it in bronze. Recognition was a problem for Best: he had too much of it from those who could offer him little, not enough of it from those who could shape him. He said the captaincy of United might have changed his life. Instead he began a pattern of departure. As the poet said: "We live our lives forever taking leave."

Best had first slipped away from the Cregagh in the summer of 1961. He was 15 years old when he got on the Liverpool ferry to go on trial at United. He had never before worn long trousers. Famously Best came back days later citing homesickness and was met by his bemused father Dickie, on July-fortnight holiday from Harland and Wolff shipyard. "That's all right, son," Dickie said, "grown men get homesick."

George soon left again for Old Trafford and after that returned to Burren Way infrequently. Now he will make one last journey from there. Looking up from the house where Dickie has lived for 56 years you can see the Castlereagh Hills. They were wreathed in snow yesterday and it is believed that this is where Best is due to go, to lie in the Roselawn cemetery beside his mother Ann. It will be a day of unspeakable pain for Dickie and family. While George's memory will shine on, to many it will also feel like the interment of part of their own lives. That is how Best affected people.

For Dickie it will be tragic. He will bury his son alongside his wife in the knowledge that both died of alcohol abuse. Almost a decade ago I met Dickie in Burren Way and as we talked on his doorstep on the way out, he sighed and said of the alcoholism that has surrounded him: "I've become an expert in something I never wanted to know anything about."

Dickie Best said then that it was George's daily regret that he had not done more to help his mother. The father had been a useful amateur footballer but George always said it was from his mother that he got his athleticism. From her son, Ann Best got the down-side of fame as much as the flickering pleasure. Later she acquired a fondness for alcohol – she did not drink before she was 40, it is said – and in October 1978 she died in the house on Burren Way. The previous day, George, now 32 and in a contractual dispute with Los Angeles Aztecs, was banned by Fifa. His disintegrating career looked to have reached a full stop.

Best left California for the Cregagh. Ann Best's funeral, if memory serves, was large. It must have been on a Saturday because along with the other 12-year-olds of Rosetta Boys we had gathered as we always did outside the shops on Greenway. We stood there with our boots in hand, preparing to go and play, and saw for the first time in the flesh the man who lit up our lives.

If it is possible to love a stranger then we loved George Best. Those of us who went to school at Lisnasharragh would always ask others who their most famous ex-pupil was – so they would ask back – and we revelled in the tales. There was the "genius" telegram sent by the scout Bob Bishop to Matt Busby, then there was the scout from Leeds United who turned up late for a trial match, but from Dickie came the best, how he listened to the famous "fifth Beatle" Benfica game on the radio in the shipyard: "I was on the night shift at the time. I turned on the radio and there was this voice saying: 'And George Best has two goals'. There was only about seven minutes gone. That was one of the most important nights for George. Afterwards the press and the locals went daft for him."

In Dickie's hand that day was a letter with a German stamp and postmark. It was addressed to "George Best. Footballer. Belfast." It was 23 years after George's last United game. "I get them all the time," Dickie said.

Then one day a lad we had not seen before joined the team. He had the flaxen mane of Rod Stewart and suddenly we were handed a new kit. Then a photographer from *Shoot* magazine appeared. Rod Stewart, it turned out, was Ian Best, youngest of George's five siblings. Ian's middle name is Busby.

But there could be only one George in the Best family. There could be only one George Best.

Guardian, 26 November 2005

Index of Contributors